BASEBALL'S
Zaniest Moments

BASEBALL'S
ZANIEST Moments

Robert Obojski

Drawings by Sandy Hoffman

Sterling Publishing Co., Inc.
New York

Library of Congress Cataloging-in-Publication Data

Obojski, Robert.
    Baseball's zaniest moments / by Robert Obojski ; drawings by Sandy
Hoffman.
        p. cm.
        Includes index.
        ISBN 0-8069-3767-X
        1. Baseball—United States—Anecdotes. 2. Baseball—United States—
Humor. I. Title.
    GV873.O26   1999
    796.357'0973 21—dc21   99-044615

10 9 8 7 6 5 4 3 2 1

Published by Sterling Publishing Company, Inc.
387 Park Avenue South, New York, N.Y. 10016
© 1999 by Robert Obojski
Distributed in Canada by Sterling Publishing
c/o Canadian Manda Group, One Atlantic Avenue, Suite 105
Toronto, Ontario, Canada M6K 3E7
Distributed in Great Britain and Europe by Cassell PLC
Wellington House, 125 Strand, London WC2R 0BB, England
Distributed in Australia by Capricorn Link (Australia) Pty Ltd.
P.O. Box 6651, Baulkham Hills, Business Centre, NSW 2153, Australia
Manufactured in the United States of America

Sterling ISBN 0-8069-3767-X

ACKNOWLEDGMENTS

We'd like to thank Ron Schwartz, president of Future Sports & Memorabilia, Inc., a baseball collectibles enterprise located in midtown Manhattan, who made it possible for me to interview dozens of baseball stars from the past and present. It was through this series of lengthy one-on-one interviews that we were able to obtain further firsthand knowledge concerning the strange directions that major league baseball sometimes takes.

Thanks also to Scott Forst and John Zazo, who are real experts in the field of New York City major league baseball and who made suggestions for particular stories that would fit the definition of "zany."

We must also thank the Port Washington, New York Public Library for answering research questions, and specifically Janet West, a knowledgeable reference librarian.

As John Donne, the great English poet, said some four centuries ago, "No man is an island, entire of itself," and in that regard it takes more than a writer to produce a book. We were bolstered by an entire cadre of Sterling Publishing professionals in the editorial, production, and business departments.

Finally, we'd like to give due credit to David A. Boehm, retired chairman and founder of Sterling, who edited all of our earlier baseball books published under the Sterling banner.

ABOUT THE AUTHOR

Robert Obojski, who has written or contributed to numerous Sterling Publishing Company books for more than 30 years, has been a lifelong "baseball addict" for twice that period of time.

Obojski got seriously hooked on baseball about 1934, when he was 4 years old and living in Cleveland, Ohio. He began listening to the Cleveland Indians' play-by-play broadcast delivered by Jack Graney, the first ex-major leaguer to do games on radio. Over a period of two decades, Obojski listened to Graney broadcast some two thousand big league games, which helped to form the foundation of his baseball knowledge. From the late 1940s through the mid-1950s, Obojski worked for the Cleveland Indians (as an electric scoreboard operator and TV statistician) and came in close contact with Graney at various pregame lunches. Graney had an intense interest in "baseball's zaniest moments."

Obojski has been following the diamond game for almost 65 years, but still learns something new every day about our national pastime. Obojski has turned out various baseball books, including *Bush League—A History of Minor League Baseball* (Macmillan, 1975), *The Rise of Japanese Baseball Power* (Chilton, 1975), and *All-Star Baseball Since 1933* (Stein & Day, 1980). He has also served as a contributing editor to the *Guinness Book of World Records* and the *Guinness Sports Record Book*.

For Sterling, he has written a variety of books on baseball, including *Baseball's Strangest Moments* (1988), *Great Moments of the Playoffs & World Series* (1988), and *Baseball Memorabilia* (1991). In addition, his *Boxing Memorabilia* was published in 1992.

CONTENTS

ZANY EVENTS

GREAT HITTERS

GREAT PITCHERS

ZANY WORLD OF BASEBALL FINANCE

ZANY EVENTS

JOE PEPITONE'S STRANGE EXPERIENCES IN THE JAPANESE LEAGUES

Joe Pepitone, a native of Brooklyn, New York, who seemed to have Hall of Fame credentials from the get-go, spent twelve tumultuous seasons in the Major Leagues—the first eight with the New York Yankees (1962–1969) and the remaining years with Houston, Chicago, and Atlanta of the National League. While with the Atlanta Braves early in the 1973 season, he became disenchanted with baseball and just plain quit.

Several Japanese teams courted Pepitone at this critical point, and, by mid-June, Pepi got the itch to play ball again. So he signed a lucrative 2-year contract with Tokyo's Yakuruto Atoms of the well-regarded Japan Central League.

He made an auspicious debut on the night of June 23, when the Atoms faced the Tokyo Giants at Korakuen Stadium before a standing-room-only crowd of more than 45,000 super-enthusiastic baseball fans. Pepitone's RBI single in the sixth inning proved to be the game's winning run as the Atoms edged the powerful Giants 2–1. In the next several games, Pepitone played without distinction and reporters kept asking him when he was going to hit a home run. He finally did blast a long homer, a shot that proved to be another game winner. It was, unfortunately, Joe Pepitone's first and last homer in Japan.

Pepitone later recounted the dramatic events surrounding that game in Hiroshima: "I experienced the scariest moments of my life on the night I hit the homer. After that game, I got into a cab and I swear that more than four hundred people surrounded the car. They started punching it and kicking it, and I thought I was finished. I had a bat with me. If I had used it, you would have seen another headline like 'Pepitone in Trouble Again.'"

The four-bagger even proved to be quite profitable. Pepitone said, "They do something in Japan I wish they'd do in the United States, though. When you hit a homer in another park, the home team gives you presents—flowers, candy, clock radios, color TVs, and other good stuff. Your own team gives you a bonus of a couple of hundred bucks. Same thing if you drive in the winning run. The next day you get an envelope with money in it."

After the Hiroshima experience, Pepitone played in a few more games and then suddenly lost his desire to play anymore. He claimed that he'd injured his right ankle in a game and required both rest and medical attention. At this point, Pepitone had appeared in a total of fourteen games, had gone to bat forty-three times, collected seven base hits (giving him a measly .163 batting average), scored only one run, and batted in only those two game-winners. He never appeared in another game.

Management didn't believe Pepitone was hurt and ordered him to play. Through an interpreter, Atoms manager Hiroshi Arakawa told Pepitone, "You're a Japanese player now. You're not an American ballplayer. You play when we tell you to play."

Pepitone said of this incident, "That really got me teed. 'I'm not a Japanese ballplayer,' I told him. 'I'm a major leaguer.'"

The interpreter assigned to Pepitone by the Atoms, an Italian-Japanese named Luigi Ferdenza, stayed close to the recalcitrant first baseman just to make sure he didn't get too far away. After all, the team had a great deal of money invested in him. "Everywhere I went, Luigi followed," Pepitone said.

About a week or so after he stopped playing, Pepitone sent his wife back home to Brooklyn and then moved in with Clete Boyer, his old New York Yankee teammate, who maintained a Tokyo apartment. Boyer, who adjusted well to Japan and Japanese baseball as the regular third baseman for Tokyo's Taiyo Whales, took Pepi under his wing, and agreed with the Atoms management that if the ankle was as seriously injured as Pepitone said it was, it should be placed in a cast.

Pepitone agreed and team doctors placed the ankle in a cast, but then strange things began to happen. Within a short time the cast was removed, not by the team doctors, and Pepi was allegedly seen dancing in several nightclubs near Tokyo's Ginza district. Just how serious the ankle "injury" was has never been clearly determined, but many felt there was reason to believe Joe Pepitone had been less than candid about the true nature of his physical condition.

The "disabled" first baseman spent his days in Boyer's apartment watching color television and calling his wife in Brooklyn. The overseas telephone charges for a month amounted to at least $3000. Boyer has consistently maintained that Pepitone still owes him a very large chuck of it. Pepitone finally decided he could not "recover" from his "injury" in time to be of any use to the Atoms for the rest of 1973 and flew back home before the end of the season. "When the plane landed in the U.S.A., I kissed the ground," Pepitone declared.

The Atoms—or the Swallows, as the team is now called—were in a quandary over the whole affair, but they remained convinced that Pepitone could still be of value to them in 1974 and publicly announced early in the year that they fully expected him to report for spring training. The Japanese still had the elusive American signed to a 2-year contract.

Spring training came and went, and nothing was heard from Pepitone. Marty Kuehnert, promotions director of the Taiheiyo Club Lions based in Fukuoka, and one of the balky Brooklynite's chief critics in Japan, commented in his monthly *Japanese Baseball Newsletter* for March 15, 1974: "The big question for 1974 is whether Pepitone will return to the Yakult Swallows... It was really a shock to most fans when Yakult announced that they thought Pepitone was coming back this year. But Pepitone is up to his old tricks, and now it's a public joke as to whether he will or will not show. Apparently, Yakult's patience has grown thin. They are threatening to sever Joe's contract if he doesn't make it over soon."

In his *Newsletter* for May 15, Kuehnert commented caustically, "Joe Pepitone has definitely been given up as a lost cause."

From his home in Brooklyn early in May, Pepitone began firing a volley of verbal salvos at Japanese baseball in general. His most scathing comments were contained in an article he wrote for the sports section of the Sunday *New York Times* for May 19, 1974. Pepitone opened his vitriolic essay by relating the unhappy thoughts he had when he was a discouraged $70,000 ballplayer (a lot of money in those days, incidentally) in the land of Nippon: "I'd wake up at three in the morning and kneel down next to the bed and pray, 'Please, God, don't let me die here.'"

Then Pepitone catalogued the misfortunes he endured in Japan during his brief tenure with the Atoms. "I just couldn't feel at home. No one spoke English, I tried to learn Japanese— right turn, left turn, straight ahead. I'd get into a cab and give directions, but if you didn't tell the driver in the exact accent, he didn't know what the hell you were talking about."

He went on to say, "But the playing part, it just wasn't major league. I had to carry my own bag. I never carried my own bag in the United States, and I wasn't going to start doing it in Japan."

Marty Kuehnert, in another of his newsletters, took Pepitone to task on the point. He wrote, "Pepitone complained that things in Japan just aren't 'Big League,' as he even had to carry his own bag. For the $70,000 Joe was paid, he should have carried the entire team's bags. It would have been more help than he gave the club on the field."

In his *New York Times* article, Pepitone complained about the high cost of living in Japan. He wrote, "If you wanted a McDonald's hamburger, it cost $5... When I moved in with Clete Boyer, we did some cooking. I stayed with Clete for a month. And you know what our grocery bill was for odds and ends like salt, pepper, and milk? It was $2000. Those bonuses just weren't paying my way."

On the subject of the game itself, Pepitone remarked, "We had these team meetings before every game, and the manager gave these terrific pep talks in Japanese. I'd stand in the corner... My heart just wasn't in this whole damn thing."

Pepitone's *Times* article cause a furor in Japan and was widely circulated throughout the country. It was reprinted in whole or in part in most of the major English language dailies, including the *Asahi Evening News*, *The Daily Yomiuri*, and the *Mainichi Daily News*. The article was also translated into Japanese for many of the country's most important daily newspaper and sports weeklies.

Before and after his *Times* article appeared, Pepitone kept himself busily occupied with appearances on a wide number of New York radio and television shows—some of which were network broadcasts—and used these as a forum to repeat his criticisms of baseball in Japan and things Japanese.

The Japanese were deeply offended by the Pepitone diatribes, particularly those directly connected with pro baseball. Some Japanese, however, found elements of raw humor in the entire affair.

We were in Japan when the Pepitone article exploded and were able to observe firsthand the reactions within the country's baseball community. At a tea with Pacific League officials in the Asahi Building in the heart of Tokyo's Ginza district, we inquired about the Brooklyn first baseman's contractual status with the Yakult Swallows. One of the executives exclaimed, "Joe Pepitone?" and then became semi-hysterical laughing and crying at the same time.

Whenever we spoke with Japanese sportswriters or television and radio baseball announcers, they would almost inevitably ask, "What sort of fellow is this Joe Pepitone anyway?"

Pepitone, of course, wasn't at the ballpark long enough in Japan for anyone to really plumb the depths of his enigmatic personality.

Later on, Pepitone tried to get a major league team to sign him, but he failed in that quest because club owners doubted his reliability. After his experience in Japan, Pepi never played professionally again.

Over the years, Pepitone faced an array of personal problems, but in the late 1980s George Steinbrenner, owner of the New York Yankees, extended the hand of friendship to Pepitone and gave him a part-time post in the team's promotions department. For over a decade now, Pepi has remained on the Yankees payroll.

In late spring 1998, we interviewed Clete Boyer at a Long Island card show and asked him if Pepitone had ever reimbursed him for the $3000 worth of telephone charges made from his apartment in the summer of '73. Boyer rolled his eyes skyward and said, "I'm still waiting for my check."

JOE PEPITONE ORDERS 2000 HAMBURGERS IN ONE FELL SWOOP AT A CHICAGO WHITE CASTLE

Shortly after we spoke with Clete Boyer we had the opportunity to interview Pepitone at length at a New York City card show.

Joe, at 57, still looks every inch the athlete and he always dresses to the nines: charcoal tailored suit, tailored shirt, fancy ties, Italian custom-made shoes, and a bit of jewelry.

We presumptuously asked, "Joe, what did that suit cost you, 2500 bucks?" Pepi answered, "Not exactly, but you're not too far off."

We then asked Pepitone of his remembrances of his experiences in the Japanese professional leagues. Pepi said, "I really wasn't too happy in Japan because I felt like I was an alien there. But I've followed the game over the years and am impressed with the fact that so many Japanese guys are now playing in the American major leagues, and several of them have become stars. The Japanese are really serious about baseball. They like to imitate American styles, and there are so many American-based companies selling their stuff in Japan, like Pepsi, Coke, McDonald's and others."

"Were the McDonald's hamburgers really going for $5 a crack when you were in Japan, as you wrote in your *New York Times* article?"

Pepitone replied, "I might have exaggerated a bit on that point, but living in Japan is expensive. You've got to remember that they have to import a lot of things necessary to keep them going."

At this point, Pepitone became quite talkative and recalled another story dealing with hamburgers and baseball. He told us, "Back in 1971, when I was with the Chicago Cubs, I really had a good year and batted over .300 for the first and only time in my career. I got along well with our manager, Leo Durocher, and became something of a celebrity in Chicago. Remember, I was basically a Brooklyn/New York guy. I was invited to lots of TV and radio shows, and one day one of the interviewers asked me what I liked best about Chicago. I said that I liked the hamburgers at the White Castles in and around the Chicago Loop. I went on and on, saying that White Castle served really terrific hamburgers.

"A few day later, I received a package from White Castle headquarters in Chicago. What did the package contain? There was a bundle of 2000 coupons, each one good for a free hamburger. How the hell could I eat 2000 hamburgers? But a couple of weeks after I received that bag full of coupons, I went down to a White Castle in the heart of Chicago's Loop district threw down all 2000 coupons on the counter and demanded 2000 hamburgers. The manager was astounded and asked me how I could possibly eat 2000 hamburgers. I said, 'Just bring out those 2000 burgers and we'll hold an open house for anyone who wants one for free.'

"Then I screamed, 'Burgers on the house, compliments of Joe Pepitone!' Within a few minutes the place was jammed. White Castle didn't have enough counter guys on duty to handle the traffic, and so they let me put on a chef's hat and apron, and I dished out hundreds of burgers. This White Castle began running out of burgers before we hit the one thousand mark, and so they had to bring in additional stuff from other White Castles in the Chicago metro area. Finally, after several hours, White Castle honored all those 2000 coupons, and everyone went home happy."

Pepitone concluded by saying, "White Castle in Chicago was really happy about this big hamburger giveaway, since this story got into all of the big Chicago newspapers and was published on all the major radio and TV stations."

As the old saying goes in press agencies, "I don't care what you say about me, but just mention my name."

BAT BOY GETS THROWN OUT OF A GAME
FOR STEALING SIGNALS

Bert Padell today operates one of the nation's largest financial management agencies for show business and sports celebrities. His firm, Padell, Nadell, Fine, Weinberger & Co., occupies two spacious floors in a major office building on New York's Upper West Side.

Current clients include Robert De Niro, Madonna, and Lou Piniella. In the past, Padell's firm has represented such stars as Montgomery Clift, Elizabeth Taylor, and Joe DiMaggio.

Padell's personal collection of show business memorabilia

rivals the assemblage of baseball collectibles that adorn his office walls.

He has personalized portraits of many stars, and his collection features copies of gold and platinum records awarded to the musical stars he represents.

From his childhood Padell has had a fascination with baseball and its players. "I wanted to get autographs from as many big leaguers as possible, and by going through issues of *The Sporting News*, I was able to get the addresses of many players. Stamps at that time cost 3¢ apiece, and in those days I had very little money to toss around. I was just a kid with limited means at the time, and the autographs I got through the mail meant a lot to me. They gave me a sense of owning something valuable. And I gained those times of value through sheer perseverance."

In January 1948, at the age of 14, Padell sent letters to the New York Giants, New York Yankees, and Brooklyn Dodgers offering his services to become their batboy. He was initially rejected by each team. Finally, however, Eddie Logan, the Giants clubhouse manager, was so impressed with the boy's intensity and love for baseball that he told the young Padell, "Tell you what, kid, you got the job as assistant visiting batboy. I'm making this position available just for you. I'll pay you $2 a game."

Padell remembers, "I walked away with tears in my eyes. I just couldn't believe that this young kid from the Bronx could become assistant visiting batboy for the famous New York Giants. On my first day of work, I met such guys as BoBo Newsom, Jack Lohrke, and Whitey Lockman. I became pals with the Giants players, and I started to catch batting practice while wearing street clothes. Mel Ott was the Giants manager at the time, and when he was fired early in the season, Leo Durocher succeeded him. When Leo spotted me catching batting practice, he told the clubhouse manager to give me a uniform. One day, the regular visiting batboy got killed in a hunting accident, and I took over his position."

Then in about mid-August, the Yankees, who had heard of Padell, asked if he could serve as their batboy for a couple of weeks while their regular batboy had to serve in an army reserve unit. Since the Giants were on the road, Padell jumped at the chance.

He says, "After the season ended, the Yankees told me they would like to make me their regular batboy for the 1949 season. I told them I couldn't do it unless I spoke to Eddie Logan first. Eddie without hesitation said it would be okay with him and was appreciative of the fact that I did ask permission. He wished me good luck. Shortly after that point, a headline appeared in the sports section of the *New York Sun* reading, 'Giants Trade Batboy to the Yankees.' They were writing about me!"

Padell spent the entire 1949 and 1950 season with the Yankees as their batboy. From that 1949 season, he recalls, "I established a close relationship with Joe DiMaggio, who was bothered by a serious Achilles' heel problem for the first half of that '49 season. I would train with him, catching flies alongside him in the outfield, pitching batting practice to him."

He recalls one game in particular from that 1949 campaign. "It was late in September and the Yankees were playing the Boston Red Sox in a crucial game that went a long way in deciding the pennant. I was positioned near the batter's circle, ready to hand a bat to a Yankee, but the umpire looked over at me and threw me out of the game for supposedly stealing signals from the Red Sox pitcher and two Boston coaches. It was the Red Sox manager Joe McCarthy, a wise old owl who first caught me in the act. Yankees manager Casey Stengel came over, laid a hand on my shoulder and said gently, 'That's all for you today, kid. Go take a shower.' As far as I know, I was the first batboy ever to be tossed out of a game."

Padell recalls those moments, which occurred in a game a half-century ago, with great fondness. "That's how close I was with the Yankees. I wanted to do everything in my power to help them in any way, and, in that game, I guess I got carried away, because I overstepped my bounds."

The Yankees went on to win the pennant by the razor-thin margin of one game over Boston, and then beat the Brooklyn Dodgers in the World Series 4 games to 1.

Padell concludes, "Those were just about the best days of my life. DiMaggio came back all the way in the last half of '49 as he averaged a lofty .346 and drove in 67 runs. The Yankees also took the pennant in 1950, this time by a three-game margin over the Detroit Tigers, and in the World Series, we beat the Philadelphia Phillies in four straight. Working two straight World Series as a batboy was the thrill of a lifetime.

"Today I run a company that employs about a hundred people, a company that has international reach, but nothing can beat those days when I was a teenager, making two bucks a game as batboy for the World Champion New York Yankees."

ROGERS HORNSBY GETS SENT BACK
TO THE "FARM"

Rogers Hornsby, considered by most baseball historians as "The Greatest Right-Handed Hitter of All Time," made his major league debut with the St. Louis Cardinals in 1915 as a skinny 19-year-old infielder. After failing to become a creditable batsman during a trial period, he was called in by manager Miller Huggins, who said, "Son, we're going to have to send you back down to the farm."

Hornsby was reported as saying, "Mr. Huggins, you don't have to send me down to a farm, because my father already owns a farm down in Texas."

Hornsby did get the message finally and he came back up to the Cardinals for the next season. By the time he finished his active career in 1937, he recorded a lifetime batting average of .358, second only to Ty Cobb's astounding .367.

Known as "The Rajah," Hornsby won the National League batting championship seven times, and reached the peak of his career in the five seasons between 1921 and 1925 when he *averaged* a phenomenal .403. In that 5-year stretch he swatted over .400 three times: .401 in 1922, .424 in 1924, and .403 in 1925.

The .424 mark remains the highest batting average achieved by a 20th-century player. Strangely enough, the Rajah did not receive the Most Valuable Player award. That honor went to the Brooklyn Dodgers fireballing pitcher, Dazzy Vance, who chalked up a 28–6 record. St. Louis Cardinals owner Sam Breadon was so incensed that Hornsby was passed over that he telephoned the league office and screamed, "What the hell must my guy do to get the MVP, hit .500?"

Hornsby remained in the game in one capacity or another until his death on January 5, 1963. He spent the preceding year as batting coach for the newly-organized New York Mets.

He always maintained, "Being sent down to the farm usually does a young player a lot of good."

KEN GRIFFEY, JR. SIGNS FOOTBALL UNDER THE MOST UNUSUAL CIRCUMSTANCES

Baseball fans often go to unusual lengths to obtain a free autograph from a diamond star, with one of the strangest attempts coming during a Sunday, August 30, 1998 game between the New York Yankees and the Seattle Mariners before a packed house of more than 50,000 screaming fans at Yankee Stadium.

In the bottom of the fifth inning a fan wearing a number 24 Ken Griffey, Jr. jersey bolted from the grandstand along the left field line directly at the Mariners center fielder. Almost immediately security guards descended upon the interloper from all sides. Griffey stood in place, hands on hips, stunned, unsure of what to expect. "You never know," he said later.

The fan proceeded to hand Griffey a regulation-size *football* and a pen and asked for an autograph, just before being tackled and heaved to the ground. As the security detail gained control of the fan, Griffey inscribed his signature on the football.

As the fan was hauled away to custody, he stretched out one free hand and Griffey handed him the ball. Alas, the souvenir was later taken away by the tightly disciplined Yankees security contingent.

Ken Griffey, Jr. has always been regarded as "fan friendly." John Sterling and Michael Kay, who were doing the radio broadcast for the Yankees, guffawed throughout the curious incident.

Incidentally, the Mariners thrashed the Yankees 13–3 in that game—and the hitting star for Seattle? Why, none other than Ken Griffey, who smacked two homers and drove in five runs!

499 PITCHES IN ONE GAME!

In a so-called "normal" major league baseball game, an average of 250 pitches are thrown in a nine-inning game, or some 125 by each team. If the game is a high-scoring one, or goes a few extra innings, the count may reach the 300 mark, or in rare cases, 350.

In rarer cases, however, the pitch count may reach stratospheric heights. A case in point came on the September 14, 1998, game played between the Detroit Tigers and Chicago White Sox at Tiger Stadium. This clash turned out to be a 12-inning marathon as Chicago edged Detroit 17–16 in a wild and woolly affair.

The game was knotted at 12–12 at the end of the regulation 9 innings, and then both clubs scored three runs in the 10th to run the game to 15–15. The White Sox blasted back-to-back homers from Ray Durham and Craig Wilson in the top of the 12th, while the Tigers were able to score only once in their half of the inning, and thus they were nosed out 17–16 in what normally appears to be a football score.

The Tigers used ten pitchers and the White Sox used eight. Their total of eighteen tied the record for most pitchers in an extra-inning game. The White Sox corps of eight hurlers threw 229 pitches, while the Tigers corps of ten moundsmen threw 270 pitches, or 499 total—a fantastic amount! That comes to at least two games' worth of pitches. The game lasted for 5 hours and 12 minutes, about twice the length of an average game.

Tabulations of pitch counts were not made until recent years, but the Elias Sports Bureau of New York (official statisticians for Major League Baseball) believe that 499 pitches is the record for any game played through 12 innings. Records for pitch counts for games played to 20 innings or so are almost impossible to arrive at.

The number of hits and runs for the Chicago/Detroit donnybrook made the pitch counts run to those high levels. Chicago batters batted out 19 base hits, while the Detroit attack came through with 22 hits. Detroit pitchers walked 11 batters, while Chicago pitchers walked only a single batsman.

The Sox starting pitcher, John Snyder, threw the first 5 innings, gave up 5 runs (4 earned), and worked his pitch count up to 92 before he was relieved. The Tigers starter, Mark Thompson, got through 4 innings, giving up 6 runs (only 2 earned) before he was sent to the showers. Interestingly, he also threw 92 pitches.

Winning pitcher for Chicago was left-hander Scott Eyre, who threw the final two innings, while the losing pitcher for Detroit was Doug Bochtler, who gave up the winning run.

Chicago's Albert Belle and Craig Wilson were the hitting stars of the game as they drove in five runs apiece. Belle banged out three doubles, to go with his two singles, and went 5 for 8. Wilson, a rookie, went 4 for 7 as he homered twice and singled twice. In that high-scoring game, Belle, a 10-year veteran, passed the 1000-RBI mark.

Jerry Holtzman, veteran Chicago sportswriter, commented, "You never know what's going to happen in a major league baseball game. Depending upon the pitching, the score might wind up at 1–0, or a football-type score at 17–16. There's no use in making pregame predictions."

ALVIN DARK TELLS JIM BOUTON, "TAKE A HIKE, KID."

Back in 1950, an 11-year-old wide-eyed youngster from Newark, New Jersey, came to New York's Polo Grounds to see the New York Giants in action. After the game, the boy, an avid baseball fan and fledgling autograph collector, stood outside the players' gate in the attempt to snag an autograph or two. Among the first players to emerge was the Giants star shortstop, Alvin Dark. The young fan approached him and said, "Mr. Dark, may I have your autograph?" Dark gave the kid a hard look and said in a gruff manner, "Take a hike, kid, take a hike."

That boy who was rebuffed by Alvin Dark eventually became a big league ballplayer himself, Jim Bouton, who achieved his greatest height as a 20-game winner for the New York Yankees.

Bouton reported this episode in his best-selling book *Ball Four*, published in 1970. Thus, Alvin Dark's put-down of a young and eager baseball fan became almost universally known. This didn't make Alvin Dark look good, and the incident was all the more incongruous since he was generally held to be a very nice guy in his long career as a star player and big league manager.

We had a chance to speak with Jim Bouton at length at a September 1998 baseball promotional event in New York and asked him if his feelings were really hurt by Dark's refusal to sign his autograph book. Without hesitation, Bouton, now 59 and still looking fit enough to pitch a few innings, replied, "Not at all. I hope I didn't give that impression in *Ball Four*. I was thrilled just by the fact that a noted major leaguer, Alvin Dark, even took the trouble to speak to me, an 11-year-old kid. I actually left the Polo Grounds happy that day!"

We were also fortunate enough to have interviewed Alvin Dark himself at a 1997 Long Island card show, and asked him about the episode. Dark replied, "I can't remember the incident. After all, it happened more than 45 years ago. Maybe I was just tired that day. I almost always signed if I had the time and if I hadn't been exhausted after playing a game in the hot sun. Remember, I was a shortstop, and that's a very physically demanding position." He went on to emphasize, "I don't want to get a bad rap, because I've always been a guy who's been able to relate to people!"

Alvin Dark has been noted as a major league player/manager. One of his ex-players told us, "Alvin Dark was a born leader. I'd run through a brick wall for him." So he didn't sign an autograph for a youthful Jim Bouton. He shouldn't be classed as a villain for that one slight lapse.

FOR BOUTON, LET BYGONES BE BYGONES

Officials at the New York Public Library recently listed Jim Bouton's *Ball Four* as "one of the most influential of a list of 100 books published in the United States during the 20th century." That list included books published on all subjects—not just on sports and baseball. Bouton recounted his baseball career's trials and tribulations. He was also critical of his New York Yankees teammates, including Mickey Mantle, one of the all-time great Yankee heroes. Many members of the Yankees nerve forgave Bouton for portraying Mickey in a bad light, and they swore never to speak to him again.

Because of *Ball Four* and its repercussions, Bouton was never invited to any of the Yankees Old-Timers' Days staged annually at around mid-season—that is, until the 1998 Old-Timers' Day staged in late July of that year. George Steinbrenner, principal owner of the Yankees, continuously enforced the "ban" on Bouton from Old-Timers' Day, although he bought the Yankees in 1973—five years after the controversial author left the Bronx Bombers.

The ice was finally broken after Michael Bouton, the ex-pitcher's son, wrote an impassioned article in the June 21, 1998, issue of the *Sunday New York Times*. The article was titled "For Bouton, Let Bygones Be Bygones," and subtitled "Son's Wish on Father's Day Is to See Dad and Yogi Stand With Old-Timers."

As soon as George Steinbrenner read the article he called the elder Bouton and invited him to attend. Jim Bouton appeared at his first Yankees Old-Timers' Day ever and for the first time in 30 years wore the pinstripes of the Bronx Bombers. Bouton said, "Wearing that Yankee uniform again brought all those happy memories back when I was a kid in his 20's pitching for the best team in baseball history. I felt like I've finally been admitted back into the family. And my son, Michael, really knows how to write."

LUKE APPLING FIELDS A COFFEE POT AT CHICAGO'S COMISKEY PARK!

Luke Appling, the Hall of Fame shortstop, had a big league playing career spanning 20 seasons (1930–1950, with a year out, 1944, for military service) and was known as a great raconteur. He was a baseball "lifer": he managed and coached a long series of major and minor league teams until his passing at the age of 84 in 1991.

Appling made sports headlines in the summer of 1985, when, at the age of 78, he slammed a home run into the left field stands at Washington D.C.'s Robert F. Kennedy Stadium during an old-timers' game. Who threw the gopher ball? Why, it was none other than Hall of Famer Warren Spahn, who was a sprightly 64 at the time. After the game Spahn said, "Appling hit the homer on a hanging curve."

About a year after Appling blasted that "senior home run," we had a chance to interview him at length at a major card show staged in Los Angeles. We asked Luke what was the strangest experience he ever had on a big league baseball diamond.

With only a moment's hesitation Appling replied, "The old Comiskey Park in Chicago was built over a rubbish dump. That means the entire baseball diamond consisted of landfill. In my first full season as a White Sox regular in 1931, we were playing the Detroit Tigers and I think it was the Tigers second baseman, Charley Gehringer, who hit a hot ground ball down to short and I dug deep into the ground in trying to pick up the ball. I didn't come up with the ball, but I did bring up a rusty old coffee pot that had been buried years before the park was completed!

"The next day the team's ground crew laid down a thick layer of fresh topsoil over the infield so that players at Comiskey could concentrate on picking up baseballs rather than rusty old trash."

BABE RUTH'S "CALLED SHOT" IN THE 1932 WORLD SERIES

The third game of the 1932 World Series still stands as one of the most dramatic clashes in the long history of the Fall Classic. The October 1 game pitted the Chicago Cubs at Chicago's Wrigley Field against the New York Yankees. New York had already won the first two games of the Series played at Yankee Stadium. Babe Ruth smashed a three-run homer off Cubs starter Charlie Root in the first inning, and in the early going, teammate Lou Gehrig also homered.

In the top of the fifth inning, with the scored tied at 4–4, Ruth faced Root again. With a count of two balls and two strikes, Ruth then seemed to gesture toward the center field bleachers, as if to indicate that's where he planned to deposit Root's next pitch. Or was he merely pointing at Root? Or was he addressing the Cubs bench with an exaggerated gesture, since the Cubs bench jockeys were teasing Ruth unmercifully?

Whatever the message, Ruth delivered on Root's next pitch. He swung viciously and the ball sailed like a rocket toward center field and then went over the bleacher wall. This titanic blast put the Yankees ahead, 5–4.

Lou Gehrig matched Ruth's two-homer by following with a drive into the right field bleachers. The back-to-back in the fifth stood up as the margin of victory as the Yankees, after trading runs with the Cubs in the ninth, prevailed 7–5.

Gehrig, the on-deck hitter as the time, obviously thought that the Babe had indeed called his shot. He said, "What do you think of the nerve of that big lug calling his shot and getting away with it?"

Charlie Root, on the other hand, strongly felt that Ruth never pointed to deep center field before the home run pitch. He said soon after the action was over, "If he had pointed to the home run landing spot, I would have knocked him down with the next pitch."

Babe Ruth himself was content to go along with the called-shot scenario, although he never really expounded upon the matter in any great detail.

In 1990, we had the opportunity to interview Billy Herman, who was the Cubs second baseman in the historic game. When we asked about Ruth's "called shot," Herman exclaimed without a moment's hesitation, "I never believed that the Babe called his shot. I was standing at second base, maybe 120 feet away from the batter's box, and though Ruth was gesticulating all over the place, I really don't think that any of his actions indicated that he would blast the ball over the center field bleachers. Still, the legend that the Babe did call the shot grew and grew. We'll never really know what was in Ruth's mind."

There's no question, however, that Game 3 broke the Cubs' spirit as the Yankees went on to win Game 4 by a 13–6 count, giving the Bronx Bombers a Series sweep. Now, more than two generations after that October 1, 1932, clash between the Yankees and Cubs, the legend continues to live on. Ruth's homer off Charlie Root remains unquestionably the greatest moment of his illustrious career and the most storied circuit blast in the entire history of the World Series. Babe Ruth played his final game in the major leagues over six decades ago, but the glory of his achievement continues to live on forever.

ZANY UMPIRING IN THE JAPANESE LEAGUES

Umpiring practices in Japan are somewhat different compared to the umpiring ways in the U.S. professional leagues. For example, in a 1973 game played at Tokyo's sprawling Korakuen Stadium, a player began punching an umpire as the result of a disputed call. Several teammates joined in on the pummeling. Then the team's manager came storming out of the dugout. What did he do? Stop the fight? Heck, no. He also began punching the beleaguered ump!

Unlike American umpires, their Japanese league counterparts change their decisions—sometimes two or three times, depending upon the arguments put forward by the players, coaches, and managers. At a June 1974 game between the Tokyo Giants and the Hanshin Tigers at Korakuen, we witnessed a 45-minute game delay because of umpire indecision. All the while, the Japanese fans remained in their seats, uncomplaining.

In 1974, Joe Lutz, a former major league player and a Cleveland Indians coach, became the first American to manage a team in Japan when he was appointed pilot of the Hiroshima Toya Carp of the Central League. Lutz resigned before the season was over. Why? Because of a controversial call at home plate that went against his team. In that call, the umpire changed his mind *three* times.

GREAT HITTERS

LARRY LAJOIE'S 1901 BATTING AVERAGE ZOOMS FROM .401 TO .422

Larry Lajoie, the great fielding, hard-hitting second baseman who played in the majors for 21 years (from 1896 through 1916), won the American League batting crown in 1901 with a purported .401 average while with the Philadelphia Athletics.

Of course, a .401 average for a full season is super, but in reality Lajoie did even better. Some 50-odd years later statisticians, led by the eagle-eyed Cliff Kachline, discovered that through mistakes in addition, Lajoie was short-changed by nine hits. He actually piled up 229 base hits, including 48 doubles, 13 triples, and a league-leading 14 homers, and that boosted his average by 21 points, from .401 to .422. That .422 still stands as the highest seasonal average by an American Leaguer. (Ty Cobb's .420 in 1911 and George Sisler's .420 in 1922 now rank second.)

After the conclusion of the 1901 season, league statisticians just didn't add up Lajoie's hit total correctly—his at bats remained the same at 543, and the nine additional base hits raised his lifetime big league average by one point, from .338 to .339.

THE STRANGE RELATIONSHIP BETWEEN WALTER JOHNSON AND TY COBB

Walter Johnson versus Ty Cobb constituted perhaps the greatest and most ferocious pitcher/batter rivalry in the history of baseball. Their careers almost totally paralleled each other's. Johnson was active from 1907 through 1927, while Cobb was active from 1905 through 1928. (Cobb spent his first 22 years with the Detroit Tigers and then played his final 2 years in the majors with Connie Mack's Philadelphia Athletics.)

Thus, these two great players confronted each other for 21 years, 1907–1927. In his first time at bat against Johnson in a

1907 game pitting the Tigers against the Senators, Cobb hit a drag bunt and beat if out for a single.

In those 21 years, Cobb faced Johnson in some 400-plus total at bats and averaged .370—three points better than his record .367 lifetime mark. Cobb knew that Johnson would never pitch him inside and thus was able to "dig in" at the plate.

Both men respected each other. In fact, they became good friends and kept in contact once their playing days were over.

Cobb's records are under constant review, especially by members of SABR's stats committee. His base hit total is usually given at 4191. When Pete Rose challenged that mark during the 1985 season, reports floated around that Cobb actually pilled up 4192 base hits. At this moment, Cobb is being credited by SABR with only 4189. As Al Capp used to say in his famed "Lil Abner" comic strip, "This is confoozin' but not amoozin."

WAS CAP ANSON THE FIRST 3000-HIT MAN?

Adrian C. "Cap" Anson, who played for the Chicago Cubs (originally known as the White Stockings) of the National League for 22 seasons, between 1876 and 1897, is generally considered to be the greatest all-around baseball star of the 19th century.

While Anson played all the positions in the game, including pitcher and catcher, he was primarily a first baseman. Most record books of the past have credited Anson with being the first major leaguer to rack up 3000 base hits. The hit total came to 3081 in 9084 official times at bat for an average of .339.

However, that hit figure is being seriously disputed, especially by John Thorn, who arguably ranks as the supreme authority on baseball as it was played in the 19th century. Thorn, a longtime committee chairman at SABR and the editor of *Total Baseball* (Warner Communications), maintains that Anson's hit total is actually 2995. Why the discrepancy? Thorn said, "There was a Chicago scorekeeper who was a red-hot Anson fan and, to guarantee Anson's batting championship, he would occasionally add a base hit here and there—hits that Anson never achieved. Those 'gift' base hits added up to 86, according to my research."

Anson, nevertheless, was a towering figure in 19th-century baseball. He began his baseball career as an 18 year old with Marshalltown, Iowa, an independent league, in 1870, and then played for five seasons in the National Association, a professional circuit that was a direct predecessor of the National League, organized in 1876 as the first true major league. In the National Association he played his first year, in 1871, with Rockford, Illinois. In the next 4 seasons he starred with the Athletics of Philadelphia.

A true leader, he managed the Chicago Cubs/White Stockings from 1879 through 1897, and then served as a non-playing manager for the New York Giants in 1898.

In his 19 years as manager of Chicago, Anson led his team up to 15 first-division finishes, including five pennants. "Big Anse," as Anson was also known, was elected to the Baseball Hall of Fame in 1939.

Still, baseball stat fanatics are still trying to determine whether or not Cap Anson was a 3000-hit guy. As far as I'm concerned, I just throw up my hands as to the inexactitude of baseball records.

ALBERT BELLE, "THE SILENT"

Albert Belle, the controversial slugger, played his first 9 years in the major leagues with the Cleveland Indians, from 1988 through 1996, before he went to the Chicago White Sox as a free agent in 1997. In his tenure with the Indians, he established a team record by slamming 242 homers, and reached his absolute peak in 1995 when he became the first big leaguer to hit 52 doubles and 50 homers.

Unfortunately, Belle was noted as a surly character who didn't sign autographs for fans, refused to speak with reporters, and on one occasion he threw a baseball directly at a fan who was seated in the bleachers. The Indians ordered Belle to receive counseling. He seemed to improve his deportment for a time, but he kept slipping back to his old ways.

Despite his negative personality, Belle developed friendships with a number of coaches and teammates. On the Indians he was on particularly good terms with coach Dave Nelson and infielder Jim Thome.

In mid-September 1998, Belle revisited his old haunts at Cleveland's Jacobs Field with his Chicago White Sox. As Belle was awaiting his turn to take pregame batting practice, Dave Nelson came up to Belle, extended his hand, and said, "How ya doin', Albert?" Belle simply turned around, refused to shake hands, and never looked at Nelson. As Nelson walked back to the Indians dugout, Thome also came up to Belle for a friendly handshake. Again, Belle shunned the gesture and turned his back on Thome without looking at him. This may seem to be strange behavior, but as the old saying goes, "A leopard never changes his spots."

MARK MCGWIRE, HOME RUN HITTER EXTRAORDINARE

During the 1998 season, Mark McGwire reached his peak as one of the premier home run hitters of all time, surpassing records established by such great sluggers of the past as Babe Ruth, Lou Gehrig, and Roger Maris.

Maris's record of 61 homers in '61 stood for 37 years until it was first broken by McGwire in 1998 and then by Sammy Sosa, outfielder with the Chicago Cubs, who also breached the Maris standard in the same '98 season. Sosa finished with 66 homers, but McGwire went on to virtually demolish the old mark when he concluded the season with an even 70 circuit clouts.

Even more incredibly, McGwire averaged 60 homers per season from 1996 to 1998—slamming a total of 180 balls out of the park. That is far and away a record. With Oakland in '96, McGwire led the National League with 52 homers, and then in '97 he hit 34 homers before being traded to the St. Louis Cards on July 31. For St. Louis, "Big Mac" homered 24 more times, giving him a total of 58. And his 70 in '98 gave him 180, or a 60 average over three seasons. Incredible!

McGwire also became the first player in history to hit 50 or more homers in three consecutive seasons. Babe Ruth did hit 50 or more homers four times, but never in three seasons in succession.

Ruth's best 3-year total came during the 1926–1928 seasons when he slammed out 47, 60, and 54 homers, respectively for a total of 161. Many baseball historians felt that record would never be broken, but McGwire's three-season total bettered the Ruth mark by 19.

The big difference between the Ruth era and the McGwire era revolves around the fact that homers were not in vogue at the time the Babe was at his peak, from 1919 until the early 1930s. (During the first half-dozen years of his career with the Boston Red Sox, from 1914 to 1919, Ruth was almost primarily a pitcher—in 1919, he began to pitch sparingly, played the outfield almost every day, and hit 29 homers in 130 games.)

Ruth, in fact, on two separate occasions, in 1920 and 1927, personally hit more homers than each of the seven other *teams* in the American League. In 1920, the "Sultan of Swat" smacked out a record 54 homers and no team in the league matched that total.

In 1927, the Bambino, at the peak of his long ball power, whacked his then record 60 homers, and in that season no single American League team managed to top that total. Philadelphia "threatened" Ruth with 56 four-baggers.

In 1998, McGwire faced competition for the National League home run crown from Chicago's Sammy Sosa. McGwire and Sosa were tied at 66 going into the final weekend of the season. While Sosa did not connect for the circuit, McGwire hit four home runs in the last two games, giving him 70.

Because there were so few authentic home run hitters in the Ruth era, the Babe really stood out in the long ball department, but McGwire does his belting in a home-run crazy period in baseball history.

MARK MCGWIRE'S SYNTHETICALLY
MARKED HOME RUN BALLS

During the 1998 home-run race between St. Louis Cardinals' Mark McGwire and Chicago Cubs' Sammy Sosa, fans became obsessed with catching the home-run baseballs hit into the grandstands by that duo, especially by McGwire, who outpaced Sosa in the homer derby for most of the time.

From a historical perspective, Sal Durante, a New York fan, became a minor celebrity after he retrieved Roger Maris' 61st home run ball in the right field bleachers at Yankee Stadium on October 2, 1961. Durante reportedly sold the historic baseball for $5000.

National League officials were cognizant of the fact that any record-breaking McGwire homer baseball would undoubtedly be worth a lot of money on the open market. As the St. Louis slugger passed the 50-homer mark, every ball pitched to him was marked with synthetic DNA to make it identifiable. Thus, there would be no chance for anyone to pass off a "fake" McGwire home run ball.

On the last day of the 1998 season, on Sunday, September 27, at Busch Stadium in St. Louis, Mark McGwire, in his final time at bat, lined his 70th home run into a deep left field luxury-box suite. After a ferocious scramble, Philip Ozersky, a 26-year-old technician at the St. Louis University School of Medicine, came up with the ball.

Within 2 weeks after gaining possession of the ball he received some four hundred inquires from dealers and collectors. Three St. Louis collectors got together and offered Ozersky a cool $1 million. Ozersky hired a lawyer to help him sort through all the offers.

The baseball is considered to be worth far more than $1 million, and now ranks as the single most valuable bit of baseball memorabilia.

One of the wackiest offers for the ball came from a man who identified himself as a distributor for a major American dollmaker. Ozersky's lawyer commented, "This guy thinks he can get a million threads out of the ball, and insert one tiny thread into a million dolls. And sell them as Mark McGwire dolls with a piece of the ball in each one. That's not all. Then he wants to put the ball back together with other thread and sell it!"

CRAZY HOME RUN STATS

Home runs were a relatively scarce commodity during the so-called Dead Ball Era, which ended in about 1919. In 1902, for example, the Philadelphia Phillies knocked only four balls out of the park, while the Pittsburgh Pirates led the National League with only nineteen! Tommy Leach of the Pirates (who completed the season with a fantastic 103–36 record to finish in first place 27.5 games over second-place Brooklyn), was the "Home Run King" in that year with a puny total of 6. All told, the eight National League teams collectively hit 98 homers.

The pennant-winning Chicago White Sox of 1906, called "The Hitless Wonders," batted a sickly .228, the league's lowest mark ever complied by an A.L. pennant winner. The Sox hit a measly 6 homers all season, the lowest figure in the majors.

The White Sox, blessed with great pitching, whipped their crosstown rivals, the Cubs, in the World Series in 1906, although their team batting average fell below the "Mendoza line" at .198. But they still outhit the Cubs, who averaged .196.

The White Sox "outdid" themselves in the home run department in 1908 when they finished a strong third with an 88–64 mark, finishing below Cleveland and first-place Detroit. The Sox hit exactly three homers, the all-time low mark for any team in major league history. Team "leaders" in home runs for the Sox were Fielder Jones, Frank Isbell, and pitcher Ed Walsh, who each hit one round-tripper.

St. Louis and Boston led the team "home run parade" in 1908 with 21 each. Nowadays, guys like Sammy Sosa can hit that many homers in a month!

In the 1909 season, the White Sox (a fourth-place finisher at 78–74) really revved up the power department as the team hit a total of four homers—not terribly good, but one better than in 1908.

The second-place Washington Senators in 1945 (87–67; they finished only 1½ games behind the pennant-winning Detroit Tigers) "led" the majors with the fewest home runs: 23. Incredibly enough, none of the homers was struck at the Senators' home park, the spacious Griffith Stadium. All came while the team was on the road. Harlond Clift paced the Washington homer "attack" with a total of eight.

The reasons for such low productions? This was a World War II year, when baseballs were generally of poor quality and didn't travel well. Plus, Griffith Stadium's dimensions were onerous—the distance from home plate to the left field bleachers was an overwhelming 405 feet, and the distance down to the right field wall was a more modest 328 feet; the wall stood at an imposing 40 feet. What is really amazing is that no Senator hit an inside-the-park homer in that big ballpark. There are some things about baseball that cannot be explained!

EDD ROUSH'S 48-OUNCE BAT

Edd Roush (1893–1988), whose career spanned the 1913–1931 period and who was one of the greatest all-around players in the National League, was such a ferocious competitor that he became known as "The Ty Cobb of the National League." Roush gained Hall of Fame election in 1962, with many baseball historians maintaining that he should have been give his bronze plaque at Cooperstown much earlier.

Roush's brilliant career was marked by one peculiarity: he used a 48-ounce bat, the heaviest bat ever used by a major league player. Contemporary players generally use bats weighing from 32 to 34 ounces, while a number even use 31-ouncers, even sluggers. The ballplayer of today feels he can gain greater bat speed with a lighter piece of lumber, enabling him to drive the baseball for a greater distance.

As Roush approached his 80th birthday, he said, "I hit very different from the way they hit today. I don't believe anyone used a bat heavier than the 48-ounce type I had. It was a shorter bat, with a big handle, and I tried to hit to all fields. Didn't swing my head off, just used a snap swing to make contact and drive the ball."

Roush retained his batting style and his 48-ounce wooden bat even though the lively ball came into being in 1919–1920 and other players went for much lighter clubs to generate more bat speed in order to hit for distance.

His tactics obviously paid off, because Edd Roush won two National League batting championships while with the Cincinnati Reds in 1917 and 1919, averaging .341 and .321, respectively. In 1967 big league games he averaged .323 and piled up 2376 base hits. While he managed only 67 home runs, he hit 339 doubles and 183 triples, the latter being a very lofty stat.

DAVE KINGMAN—FOUR TEAMS IN ONE SEASON!

David Arthur Kingman, a 6-foot–6-inch, 220-pound home run slugger, slammed out 442 circuit blasts during his checkered 16-year big league career (1971–1986), and that gives him the distinction of having the most homers for a player *not* in baseball's Hall of Fame.

Throughout his tenure in the big leagues, Kingman was noted for not speaking with reporters and being generally hostile to the press as a whole. Early on, after he reached the majors with the San Francisco Giants in 1971, he claimed he

was badly misquoted after giving out a series of interviews. And because of his generally ornery personality, Kingman went from one team to another, playing for a total of seven teams in both major leagues.

He was signed out of the University of Southern California by the San Francisco Giants and he debuted with the parent club late in the 1971 season. Just before the start of the 1975 campaign, Kingman was sold to the New York Mets. By that time he had worn out his welcome with the Giants.

Big Dave remained with the Mets for the entire 1976 season, and then in '77 he really hit the jackpot for changing teams. In that year he played for exactly four of them. He went to the San Diego Padres in a June 15 trade, then on September 6 he was sold on waivers to the California Angels. His tenure with the Angels lasted for exactly 9 days because on September 15 he was sold to the New York Yankees. Yes, he did remain with the Yanks for the remainder of the season, 2 whole weeks. Baseball historians found that seeing service with four big league teams within a single season at least ties a record.

The Yankees had no interest in signing Dave for 1978, and so the big slugger signed with the Chicago Cubs, where he remained, remarkably enough, for three full seasons.

Though he was on the disabled list for nearly a month in '78, Dave still managed to hit 28 homers in 119 games. In '79, when many baseball experts said that Dave was nearing the end of the road, he surprised everybody by having a "career year" as he led the league with 48 homers and 115 runs batted in while averaging a solid .288—all career highs for him. Dave's fortune declined in 1980 as he went on the disabled list three times, but when he was on the diamond he did play well, batting .278 in 81 games with 18 homers.

The Cubs soured on Kingman for a variety of reasons, particularly because of one grisly incident. He took a strong dislike to one female Chicago baseball reporter and expressed his displeasure with her writing by placing an expired rodent in her handbag.

Dave went over to the New York Mets at the beginning of 1981, and though he was happy about getting back to his old club, he again spent a bit of time on the DL, and was also benched at various times for striking out too much. Though he averaged .221 in 100 games, he did manage to slam 22 homers. The Mets knew that Kingman was a big gate attraction, a real threat at the plate. Moreover, fans liked to see his 450- to 500-foot "homers" into the stands during batting practice.

"King Kong" Kingman tried mightily to mend his ways in '82, and he kept himself off the bench by showing sporadic and game-winning bursts of power. While he averaged a skinny .204 (going 109 for 535 in 149 games), he led the league with 37 circuit blasts and drove in 99 runs. No other player has led the league in homers with that low an average. A free- and sometimes wild-swinger, Dave struck out a league-leading 156 times. Dick Young, then a baseball writer for the *New York Daily News*, and long one of Dave's severest critics, called him "King Kong Kingman, The Strikeout King."

Kingman went on to have a career worst season in '83 as he "rode the pines" for long periods. He batted less than his weight, .198 in 100 games, and homered only 13 times.

He certainly wasn't ready to quit baseball at that point. After his release by the New York Mets, he signed with the Oakland Athletics in 1984, and remained with the A's for three full seasons, retaining his reputation as an authentic home run threat. In those 3 years he hit exactly 100 homers—35, 30, and 35, respectively. His 1984 stats were particularly good: he averaged a strong .268 and knocked in 118 runs. Kingman was miffed that he didn't make the American League All-Star team in 1984, although he did play in the 1976 and 1980 All-Star games.

After being released by the A's following the '86 season, Kingman still had visions of reaching the magic 500 home run mark, and tried making a comeback in July '87 by signing with Phoenix of the Triple AAA Pacific Coast League. But after 20 games, with a sub-standard .203 average and only 2 homers, Dave hung up his uniform for good.

There are still those baseball writers who are long ball aficionados who feel Kingman is Hall of Fame material, despite his .236 lifetime batting average in the majors. They also point to his 1210 runs batted in and his home run ration of 6.6% (measured against official times at bat)—a stat good enough to give him a fifth-place spot on the all-time list among retired players. Dave's detractors point to his 1816 strikeouts—another fifth-place all-time rating.

We had the opportunity to interview Dave Kingman in October 1998. Frankly, we've never encountered a more affable and approachable interviewee. Said Kingman, "I may not have liked sportswriters when I was playing, and though I may have been a bit tough to get along with, I've always felt I was a decent person. Maybe I got a less than excellent reputation early in my career, but I was young, maybe a bit immature, but I have grown up. Remember, there are real pressures in playing big league baseball. Some basically excellent players fold because they cannot handle the pressure and play at their best before big and noisy crowds. I've felt that most baseball fans are fair and decent to the players, but the noisy boo-birds can get under your skin and warp your personality. By the same token, baseball writers in general are decent guys, but there are those who rip you all the time, and that kind of stuff can affect you. In general, I had a good career and have no regrets. Playing big league baseball is a rough and tumble profession."

AVERAGE LIFE OF A MAJOR LEAGUES BASEBALL IS ONLY SIX PITCHES!

During major league baseball's so-called "Stone Age," the late 1870s up to the turn of the century, a ball stayed in the game until it became so discolored, or even misshapen, that it had to be thrown out for a replacement. There are even confirmed reports that a single baseball was used for an entire game back in those old days! In fact, the use of beat-up balls continued to be a practice in the big leagues up to around the World War I period.

Edd Roush, a National League outfielder, heavy hitter, and Hall of Famer, often spoke of mashed-up baseballs being used in championship games. He spoke of this in great detail in an interview that appeared in Lawrence S. Ritter's landmark book *The Glory of Their Times*, published in 1966.

Roush, who played in the majors from 1913 to 1931, mostly with the Cincinnati Reds and New York Giants, recalled, "Until 1919, they had a dead ball. Well, the only way you could get a home run was if the outfielder tripped and fell down. The ball wasn't wrapped tight and lots of times it'd get mashed on one side.

"I've caught many a ball in the outfield that was mashed flat on one side. Come bouncing out there like a jumping bean. They wouldn't throw it out of the game, though. Only used about three or four balls in a whole game. Now they use 60 or 70."

Roush had that just about right. A recent study by Major League Baseball indicates that the average ball has a life of only about six pitches in a game. Rawlings Sporting Goods, Inc., based in Saint Louis, supplies all the baseballs used by the thirty teams making up the American and National Leagues. Those thirty teams gobble up 720,000 baseballs every season, according to Rawlings. A baseball retails for $6, but the major leagues buy them up at wholesale prices.

Mark McGwire, the St. Louis Cardinals slugger, hits a lot of homers out of the park, but even if he connects 60 or 70 times in a season, that will amount to only a fraction of the baseballs lost in action. And that says nothing of the many baseballs McGwire hits out of the park in batting practice. McGwire, in fact, draws crowds of fans who want to see him blast baseballs into the bleachers and over the stands in batting practice.

Rawlings Sporting Goods also supplies baseballs to most of the minor league teams, as well as to thousands of amateur teams scattered across the United States. Virtually all of the Rawlings baseballs are made overseas, particularly in Haiti, where the company takes advantage of low-priced labor. Baseball manufacture is labor intensive because the balls must be hand-stitched. Neither Rawlings or any other company has been able to develop machinery to stitch baseballs on an assembly-line basis. The work must be done with human hands.

GREAT PITCHERS

WHEN IS A RECORD NOT REALLY A RECORD?

When George Edward "Rube" Waddell, the brilliant but eccentric Philadelphia Athletics left-hander, struck out a supposed total of 343 batters in 1904 (Rube went 25–19 in 384 innings of work), that posting stood as a major league record for decades.

Fast-forward to the 1946 season when Bob Feller, fireballing right-hander of Cleveland Indians, went on a strikeout binge and wound up with 348 Ks in 371 innings of work as he went 26–15.

Did Feller set a new record? Apparently he did, but whoa! Researchers at the weekly *Sporting News*, led by editor Cliff Kachline, checked through all Philadelphia Athletics box scores of 1904 when Waddell pitched, and discovered that Rube actually fanned 349 batters. The 349 figure was duly recognized, relegating Feller's strikeout total to second place. (Subsequently, of course, Waddell's record was broken, first by Sandy Koufax with 382 Ks in 1965, and then by Nolan Ryan with 383 Ks in 1973.)

Kachline commented on this strange statistical phenomenon: "Official scorers over the years turned in scoresheets with mistakes in them, often simple mistakes like addition. Researchers have gone over these erroneous scoresheets and made the necessary corrections. Thus, the stat has to be changed. Scorers erred because they were usually under deadline pressure. For example, newspapers wanted them in a hurry so they could be printed in a particular edition."

Kachline also mused, "Sometimes, the official scorers, who were working sportswriters, did not always show up to the game in any kind of condition to do accurate work. No wonder so many mistakes were made."

THE QUESTION OF WALTER JOHNSON'S VICTORY TOTAL

When fireballing right-hander Walter Johnson retired following the 1927 season after spending 21 years with the Washington Senators, his victory total was given at 413 against 279 losses. Only Cy Young, who won 511 games, has a higher big league victory total than Johnson.

Strangely enough, however, Walter "Big Train" Johnson hadn't finished winning ballgames. Several years after his death in 1946, a number of researchers discovered, by checking all of the box scores of games in which Johnson pitched, that the scorers did not give him credit for three additional victories. Now all the standard references give Johnson 416 total wins.

Johnson's grandson Henry W. Thomas wrote an excellent and well-received biography on the "Big Train" in 1996, appropriately titled *Walter Johnson: Baseball's Big Train*, and said with great family pride, "My granddad was such a great pitcher that he won three major leagues games after he died."

Thomas added that the "Big Train" also struck out 11 batters after his passing since his K total was revised from 3497 to 3508.

Walter Johnson was reputed to have thrown a baseball as fast or faster than any other pitcher in baseball history. He was called "Big Train" because it was said that his best pitch traveled faster than any locomotive in existence. Radar guns were not invented during Johnson's era, but most baseball experts who saw "Big Train" in action said they've never seen a pitcher who could match his speed. In today's terms, his fastball traveled a tad over 100 miles per hour. No human could match that kind of speed.

In his 458-page tome on his grandfather, Henry Thomas repeatedly emphasized again that Walter Johnson made it a practice never to throw close inside to a batter. With his speed, Johnson, one of the true gentlemen of the game, never wanted to hit a batter with his blazing fastball.

Henry Thomas wrote, "If Granddad had pitched tight like so many pitchers of today—including Don Drysdale, who pitched in tight continuously—he could have become a 500-game winner. He never wanted to take a chance of hitting a batter with all that speed. If Walter Johnson threw inside as a matter of strategy, batters would be afraid to dig in. He gave the batters an even chance by not intimidating them, and he still established himself as one of the greatest pitchers of all time."

Two other stats reflect the true greatness of Johnson as a moundsman: his ERA stands at a very skinny 2.17 (good for seventh best on the all-time list), and he threw 110 shutouts, and that is *the record*. He threw only one no-hitter on July 1, 1920, against the Boston Red Sox.

EXTRAORDINARY MOUND FEATS BY EXTRAORDINARY PITCHERS

Nowadays most big league pitchers "baby" their arms. In the old days, most major league teams utilized a four-man rotation; now it's a five-man rotation. That is, hurlers today work every fifth day instead of every fourth day. And these five starters are backed up by a "relief crew" of seven additional pitchers.

The seven relievers are classed into categories: "long men," "set-up men," and "closers." Often times, a reliever will be thrown into the fracas with the purpose of blowing out only a single batter. That "specialist" may be a left-hander whose job it is to get out a left-handed batter in a critical situation late in the game.

Today, moundsmen are taken out of a game if their "pitch count" reaches a certain number of pitches. Some starters are limited to as few as 100 pitches before they're taken out of a game. Very seldom is a starter allowed to hurl as many as 130 pitches per game. A relief pitcher, who often is called upon to "put out fires" two or three times a week, is limited to 30 or perhaps 40 pitches at most. The closer usually comes in to shut down the other side for a single inning. That is true of famed closers like Dennis Eckersley and John Franco. When they go past one inning in a closer situation they make news.

Strangely, there are now cases where a moundsman appears in about as many games as innings pitched. Take the case of Eckersley, one of the premier relievers of the past 10 or 12 years: In 1993 with the Oakland Athletics, he appeared in 64 games and chalked up only 67 innings pitched; he did have 36 saves—a very good performance. Then with Oakland in 1995, he appeared in 52 games, with only 50 1/3-innings pitched, and a strong 29 games saved. With the St. Louis Cardinals in 1997, he got into 57 games and hurled only 53 innings. He recorded 36 saves, and though his won-lost record was a less-than-mediocre 1–5, that stat doesn't mean all that much. Relievers are paid according to games saved.

John Franco's stats in respect to games played and innings pitched are similar to Eckersley's. While with the New York Mets in 1991, he appeared in 52 games and threw in 55 1/3-innings to go with 30 saves; in 1996 with the Mets, he got into 51 games and threw 54 innings, with 28 saves. Franco is the prototypical closer who rarely goes beyond a one-inning stint. Thus, complete games have become a relative rarity in the big leagues.

Greg Maddux, the star Atlanta Braves right-hander, led the National League in complete games in 1993, 1994, and 1995 with 8, 10, and 10, respectively—low numbers for the leader in that category.

Back in the old days, a reliever was often brought in with the idea that he would finish the game for the starter who was knocked out of the box. In general, lengthy relief appearances have almost gone the way of the carrier pigeon.

Eddie Rommel, the old Philadelphia Athletics star right-hander, spent the last couple of seasons in his 13-year major league career (1920–32) as a reliever, and he chalked up what is generally thought to be the longest relief assignment in big league history.

That came in a July 10, 1932, game against the Cleveland Indians. Athletics starter Lew Krausse was taken out of the game in the first inning when he gave up 3 runs and 4 hits. With two outs, Rommel came in to put out the fire. What finally happened was that this turned out to be one of the most unusual and highest-scoring games in major league history. This wild and woolly game lasted for 18 innings before the Athletics won by a fat 18–17 score!

Strangely, Rommel was allowed to "go the distance," and he gained the victory with his "tight" relief pitching. In 17 1/3-innings of work, he allowed 14 runs and 29 base hits. Clint Brown, the Indians starting pitcher, was relieved in the late innings by Willis Hudlin and Wesley Ferrell. In this 18-inning marathon, the Indians stroked 33 base hits while the A's hit safely 25 times for the astounding total of 58.

Johnny Burnett, the Indians second baseman, established a record that still stands after nearly 70 years: 9 base hits in a single game in 11 at bats. Indians second baseman Billy Cissell had 4 hits, while first baseman Eddie Morgan hit safely 5 times.

For the A's, first baseman Jimmie Foxx picked up 6 hits in 9 at bats, while left fielder Al Simmons went 5 for 9. No doubt about it, the Indians and the A's had their hitting clothes on during that hot July day in 1932.

The Indians and Athletics were tied 15–15 after 15 innings, but both teams scored a brace of runs in the 16th to knot the score at 17–17. Then the A's scored single runs in the top of the eighteenth to put the game away at 18–17, a football-type score. Nowadays, a game of that length would require about six or so pitchers on each side, but in this monumental clash only five moundsmen saw action.

Rommel had a reputation for being a workhorse, since he had a string of games to his credit where he pitched well beyond nine innings. In an April 13, 1926, game against Washington, for example, he hooked up in a pitching duel with the great Walter Johnson. The Senators squeaked out a 1–0 victory over the Athletics in fifteen innings. Both pitchers went the distance, of course. That wouldn't happen today, because pitchers are rarely allowed to go beyond nine innings. Later on in his career, Rommel became an American League umpire and served for twenty-three seasons (1938–1960) as an A.L. arbiter.

During our years with the Cleveland Indians in the 1950s, we had the chance to speak with Eddie Rommel on several occasions. He was an imposing figure, standing about 6 foot 2 inches and weighing an athletic 200 pounds.

We asked Rommel why pitchers of his era were often able to work so many innings at a single stretch. He answered, "When I broke into pro baseball back in 1918 with the Newark Bears of the International League, we were just coming out of the 'dead ball' era and getting a new, juiced-up, lively ball that made it easier it hit homers. Even after the lively ball came into being in about 1919–20, a lot of hitters liked to continuing to 'slap' the ball and tried more than anything to 'place' relatively short hits. Ty Cobb was basically a slap hitter—I pitched to him many times, and he rarely tried to go for homers.

"Remember, Cobb became a little jealous of Babe Ruth hitting all those homers, and in 1925 Ty said, in effect, 'There's no real trick to hitting homers.' Then he set out to prove his point. In back-to-back games against the St. Louis Browns at Sportsman's Park early in May that year, Ty changed his batting style by taking a full swing. He hit three home runs in the first game, and two more on the following day, giving him five for the two games."

Historians indicated that Cobb was unlucky to hit seven homers in 2 days. Two of his shots missed the roof at Sportsmen's Park and dropped for doubles. Rommel went on to say that after that spectacular 2-day performance, Cobb went back to his old batting style, consisting of a snap swing and a quick chop so that he did not have to set himself. That made him able to shift quickly so he could meet any kind of pitch—high, low, inside, outside. The snap swing enabled him to meet the ball squarely even while he was shifting.

Rommel concluded his observations by saying that since pitchers in his era didn't have to worry all that much about game-breaking home runs, they didn't have to absolutely have to "bear down" on every pitch. He said, "We could pace ourselves." Rommel also emphasized that back in his playing days, pitchers objected to being relieved and strove to remain in the game as long as possible. Thus, starters of that era rolled up more innings per season generally than today's moundsmen. And by the same token, relievers didn't like being relieved, and that's one of the reasons he threw that famed 17⅓-inning, 29-hit relief performance on the afternoon of July 10, 1932.

BOB FELLER DIDN'T COUNT HIS PITCHES

From the time Bob "Rapid Robert" Feller broke in with the Indians in mid-season in 1936 as a 17 year old who could heave the baseball 100 miles per hour, he was hailed as the Tribe's best pitcher since old Cy himself. When Feller enlisted in the navy on December 9, 1941 (2 days after Pearl Harbor), he had already won 107 games for Cleveland (against 54 losses). No pitcher in baseball history had piled up that many victories that quickly—not even Cy Young himself. Before Feller joined the U.S. Navy, many baseball historians thought that the fireballing right-hander had an even chance of at least approaching Cy Young's monumental victory total. However, Feller's navy duty took him away from baseball for 3½ years. He was discharged from the navy toward the end of July 1945. In his first game back, he defeated the Detroit Tigers 4–2 and struck out 12. He obviously regained his old form.

Feller went 5–3 for the last couple of months in the '45 season, and then in 1946 he turned in an almost unbelievable iron-man performance as he rolled up a 26–15 record for the sixth-place Indians. The Indians posted a mediocre 68–86 record that season; thus, Feller won nearly 40% of the team's games.

In 48 games, he pitched an almost incredible 371 innings, gave up a sparing 277 base hits, and came up with a skinny ERA of 2.18. He made 42 starts and led the league in complete games with an amazing 36. He struck out 348 batters, a figure that was thought to be a record, but later Rube Waddell's strikeout total with the 1904 Philadelphia Athletics was raised to 349 (see page 54).

Feller was thrown into relief situations six times so that he could pitch extra innings in order to have a better chance at breaking Rube Waddell's one-season strikeout record. No starting pitcher in the current era of baseball was ever called upon to go into a game as a reliever.

Still, Feller's regular season stats give only a part of his over-strenuous pitching activities in 1946. Feller wanted to recover the lost baseball income during the nearly 4 years he served in the U.S. Navy. He organized a 30-day nationwide barnstorming tour composed of two teams consisting of major leaguers, plus top players from the Negro professional leagues. During that barnstorming tour, Feller pitched at least 60–70 innings in competition, and thus for the whole of 1946, he threw something like 450 innings. And that's not to say how many innings he threw in spring training in 1946. Nowadays no pitcher would follow a schedule that outrageously arduous.

Bob Feller would have piled up even more impressive lifetime pitching stats had it not been for a strange accident that occurred in a game he was pitching against the Philadelphia Athletics in June 1947. He fell off the mound—it was a bit

slippery since it had been raining that day—and injured his right pitching shoulder.

From that point on, Rapid Robert was never quite the same again. He would never be able to throw those 100-plus mile-per-hour fastballs. But, despite the injury, Bob had a lot of baseball savvy and retained enough good stuff to remain in the majors for another decade. He finished the '47 season at 20–11, and then struggled through the Indians' 1948 pennant with a 19–15 record. While he led the league in strikeouts with 164 in 280 innings, that was well under par for Rapid Robert.

Feller's great ambition was to win a World Series game, but he failed in that quest because of one of the strangest plays in the history of the "Fall Classic." Bob started Game 1 against the Boston Braves at Boston. The game was scoreless through the first 7 innings. Then, in the bottom of the eighth, Bill Salkeld singled to open the inning and Braves manager Billy Southworth sent Phil Masi in to run for him. Mike McCormick sacrificed and Eddie Stanky drew an intentional walk. Feller then attempted to pick off Masi, who had taken a big league off second. Feller whirled around and fired a bullet to shortstop-manager Lou Boudreau, who cut in behind the runner. Masi slid back and was called safe by base umpire Bill Stewart, although Boudreau protested vehemently that he had made the tag well before the runner had reached the bag. Pitcher Johnny Sain then flied out, but Tommy Holmes came through with a single, drive in Masi. That was the only run of the game as Boston won the 1–0 squeaker. Films of the play revealed that Boudreau had tagged Masi out before the latter had gotten within 2 or 3 feet of second base.

Feller told us in a 1997 interview, "That was a strange call, all right. Stewart made a mistake because he was not in position to see the tag out. That's the breaks of the game." Feller can be very philosophical about misadventures in baseball. In going the distance, Feller allowed only two hits, walked only three, and struck out two.

After Bill Stewart retired from the National League umpiring crew several years later, he began a new career as a major league scout. And who hired him to that post? Why, none other than the Cleveland Indians. Strange.

In the '48 World Series, Feller got a second chance to win a Series game. In Game 5 at Cleveland Stadium, a clash that drew a standing-room-only crowd of 86,288 (then a record crowd for *any* big league game), Bob was sent to the showers in the inning with only one man out. He gave up 7 runs on 10 hits, as the Tribe took an 11–5 drubbing. The Indians did take the Series 4 games to 2, with Rapid Robert being the team's only losing pitcher against the Braves.

Feller went 15–14 and 16–11 in the 1949 and 1950 season, respectively—not bad, but not approaching Rapid Robert's past greatness. In 1951, he enjoyed an extraordinary season as he posted a glittering 22–8 record. Many sportswriters were ready to write off Feller as a front-line pitcher at this point in his career, and though Feller's fastball was no longer in the 100-mile-per-hour zone, he made up for it in craftiness. He struck out only 111 batters in 250 innings of work, but he led the American League in wins and in winning percentage with a .733 posting. Even at that fairly late point in his career, Bob threw 16 complete games in 34 starts (more CGs than most league leaders achieve today), including a no-hitter against Detroit on July (the third no-hitter in his career).

Toward mid-season, Feller was involved in just about the strangest of all games in his 18 years as an Indian—a game against the Philadelphia Athletics. The Indians had their hitting clothes on in that clash, and they whomped A's pitchers for 21 runs. The Athletics were no pushovers in the hitting department that day either, as they scored 9 runs. Did Feller get any relief in that slugfest? Absolutely not! He went the distance in picking up the victory. Today, if Feller has been pitching, he would have been yanked after 5 or 6 innings, just enough to get credit for a win, and the members of the relief corps would have been called in to mop up.

In our 1997 interview with Bob, we asked him why he was permitted to remain on the mound for the entire game where he was getting shelled. He answered, "I asked our manager, Al Lopez, to keep me in the game for a solid purpose. I was experimenting with a couple of new pitches, and I wanted to throw them in game conditions, so it didn't make any difference if I allowed Philadelphia to score a few additional runs, for we had the game wrapped up from the get-go. I know that you can't get away with stuff like that today, but I was glad to work out those pitches in competition and that did help me a lot down the road. And I've got to give credit to Al Lopez who allowed me to work on those new pitches. And I'm glad to see that Al made it into the Hall of Fame as a manager." Bob concluded, "I must have thrown at least 175 pitches in that game, but then nobody was counting."

Feller dropped to a 9–13 record in 1952, went 10–7 in 1953, and then roared back in 1954 where he posted a 13–3 winning season as a "spot starter." In 19 starts, he threw 9 CGs—not bad. That was the year when the Indians established a major league record for most victories in a season—111 wins against 43 losses.

Feller thought he had another shot at winning his first World Series game against the New York Giants, who finished the season at a comparatively modest 98–59. Unfortunately, the Giants swept the Indians in four straight games with Bob Lemon, Early Wynn, and Mike Garcia taking the losses (Lemon two of them). Manager Lopez had scheduled Feller to pitch the fifth game, but since there was no necessity for a fifth game, Bob never got to pitch in the Series. Feller, philosophical as ever, said, "Stranger and worser things have happened to me before and since. I'm not going to worry about things that I have little or no control over."

Feller wound up his career in the 1955 and 1956 seasons as a spot starter and reliever, and in his 18 years in the majors he came up with a lifetime record of 266 victories and 162 defeats. Through the late 1960s, his strikeout total of 2581 ranked fourth on the all-time list.

While Feller may not have won a World Series game, he did participate in five All-Star games and went 1–0, having been the winning pitcher in the 1946 clash at Fenway Park when the American League clobbered the Nationals 12–0.

Bob Feller certainly wasn't through with baseball after he threw his last pitch for the Cleveland Indians. He continued to appear at old-timers' games and special exhibitions and kept hurling those balls toward the plate into the early 1990s, when he was past 70 years old—or "70 years young," to be more exact in our choice of words. Moreover, he still does his own yard work at his large home in Gates Mills, Ohio, near Cleveland.

DAVID WELLS—A SUPER BABE RUTH FAN

New York Yankees left-handed pitcher David Wells, who helped the Bronx Bombers take the 1998 American League pennant and the World Series crown with an 18–4 regular season record (including throwing a perfect game), has long been noted as a super Babe Ruth fan.

When Wells joined the Yankees in 1997, he asked to wear Babe's retired number 3. When that request was denied, he settled for number 33. From that point, he purchased one of Ruth's game-worn caps at auction for $35,000, and wore it in a 1998 game against the Cleveland Indians. Wells is known in baseball circles as a free spirit.

THE ZANY WORLD OF BASEBALL FINANCE

HALL OF FAMERS' SALARIES BEFORE
THE AGE OF TELEVISION

Back in the so-called "good old days," most big league baseball players, even the biggest stars, hustled around to find temporary jobs in the off-season. During the 1940s and 1950s, many of the game's biggest stars, Hall of Famers, held everyday jobs. Duke Snider, Brooklyn Dodgers outfielder, carried mail from the Brooklyn post office during the holiday period; Stan Musial, St. Louis Cardinals outfielder/first baseman, worked as a clerk in his father-in-law's grocery store in Donora, Pennsylvania; Phil Rizzuto, New York Yankees shortstop, worked as a salesman in a New York men's clothing store; Mike Garcia, Cleveland Indians, worked in a Cleveland dry cleaning shop and then bought the business; Bob Feller, Cleveland Indians, sold insurance and then opened his own insurance company (which eventually went bankrupt); Early Wynn, Washington Senators, Chicago White Sox, and Cleveland Indians, was a construction laborer and then head of his own construction company in Alabama; and Carl Furillo, Brooklyn Dodgers, elevator repairman, Manhattan. We could list countless other stars who had to take on a variety of jobs following their playing careers, and those who had to work at odd jobs in the off-season in order to provide for their families.

It's been only within the past generation or so that baseball salaries have skyrocketed. Nowadays a player who signs a big multi-year contract is usually financially set for life.

We can state the reason for the almost geometric increase in baseball in one single word: Television. Back when baseball games were first televised in the late 1940 and early 1950s, there were many baseball experts who maintained that TV would "kill" attendance at games. These so-called "experts" said, "Why would anyone go to a game if he could see it for free on TV?" It so happened that TV got many millions of new fans interested in the game, with box office receipts zooming as a result.

Back during the 1920s and 1930s when ballgames were broadcast on radio, revenues from that source were almost inconsequential. In many cases, major league teams waived potential broadcast fees because they were happy just to get the free publicity.

The Cleveland Indians received their first "big" TV contract from station WXEL in 1951. That contract called for WXEL to broadcast all of the Indians' seventy-seven home games, plus six games on the road. For those eighty-three games, the Indians received $250,000—a lot of money in those days; in fact, enough money to cover more than half the player salaries.

Minimum salaries were not agreed upon until toward the late 1940s. When Jackie Robinson, the first black player in the major leagues, was promoted from the Montreal Royals of the International League in 1947 to the Brooklyn Dodgers under general manager Branch Rickey, he was given a $5000 contract—the big league minimum at the time. Player salaries before that time were generally paltry.

Then there's Jeff Heath, a Cleveland Indians outfielder from 1936 to 1945. He continuously complained about having to play for "peanuts." After he hit .343 and drove in 112 runs for Cleveland in 1938, he was given a contract for the 1939 campaign for about $3000—the equivalent of a Cleveland public school teacher's salary at the time.

After Heath finished his big league career with the Boston Braves in 1949, he signed a contract with the Pacific Coast League's Seattle Rainiers in 1950 worth $25,000—the highest salary by far he had ever received in baseball. In fact, no minor league player up to that point was given that type of generous contract.

Baseball salaries during the Depression era of the 1930s were generally very low, even for the biggest stars. Frank "Lefty" O'Doul led the National League in batting in 1932 while with the Brooklyn Dodgers. He averaged a fat .368. Did he get a raise for that performance? No. He was cut $1000, down from $8000 to $7000, but he still ranked among the top-paid big leaguers.

Lou Boudreau, star shortstop of the Cleveland Indians, who as a brilliant sophomore in 1940 played in every one of the team's 155 games, averaging a solid .295, drove in 101 runs, and led American league shortstops with a .986 fielding percentage. For that grand effort Boudreau played under a contract calling for the munificent sum of $5000—which amounted to little more than $30 per game.

Indians' owner Alva Bradley, a business tycoon with interests in myriad industries, felt guilty about that contract, so he gave Boudreau a $2000 bonus at season's close. Then Bradley doubled Boudreau's salary to $10,000—making him one of the higher-paid players in the big leagues.

MIKE PIAZZA AND THE TERMINAL TOWER

Sometimes the cost of player salaries becomes a little too steep, even for a multi-billionaire like Rupert Murdoch. Early in 1998, Mike Piazza, the Dodgers star catcher, demanded a 6-year contract, calling for a cool $100 million. Murdoch declined to offer such an obscene contract like that one and Piazza eventually wound up with the New York Mets before the '98 season got too far along. The Mets offered Piazza $85 million for six seasons, which added up to just over $14 million per year and would have been the richest baseball contract in history. Piazza felt he was justified in asking for a nine-figure contract because with the 1997 Dodgers he had perhaps the greatest hitting year of any catcher in the history of the diamond game. In 152 games, he averaged a lofty .362, swatted 201 base hits, including 40 homers, and drove in 124.

However, the Dodger organization felt that Piazza, at age 30, would be vulnerable to injury as an everyday catcher, and that he might have a hard time fulfilling the extent of any overblown contract. Piazza was booed throughout the 1998 season by fans in most of the National League for his outrageous salary demands, but he took the jeering in stride as he rolled up another good year, batting .329 in 151 games, with 184 hits, 32 homers, and 111 runs batted in.

$100,000,000 is an enormous amount of money, especially when the sum is considered as a long-term contractual commitment to a baseball player. Consider Cleveland, Ohio, in connection with a massive downtown building project completed in 1930–31. The project featured the Terminal Tower (52 stories and 708 feet high, the second-tallest building in the U.S. outside of New York City), plus four other solid 20-plus–story structures, including the Midland Building. It cost a total of $100,000,000—a massive amount of money in those days. Sure, the dollar is different today than it was two generations ago, but Mike Piazza demanding Terminal Tower money is zany!

GEORGE "SHOTGUN" SHUBA: "I'D SETTLE FOR THE LICENSING FEE"

George "Shotgun" Shuba, who played for the Brooklyn Dodgers from 1948 to 1955 and was the first National Leaguer to hit a pinch-hit homer in the World Series (in the '53 Series against the New York Yankees), discussed baseball salaries at length at a New York City card show. He said, "When I played, there were very few fringe benefits. Sure, some of the big stars, like Stan Musial, Yogi Berra, Ted Williams, Joe DiMaggio, and Bob Feller, made pretty fair money from commercial endorsements, but for the average player there weren't all that many opportunities to make money on the side. If I had the chance, I'd like to get a coaching job for a big league team, and I'd work for free. I'd just settle for the licensing fee."

The Major League Players Association has an agreement with Major League Baseball to share all licensing fees for the use of the MLB logo as well as individual team logos on commercial products. The royalty fee is currently pegged at about 8%. Thus, if a manufacturer retails a jacket bearing the MLB logo, or a team logo, for $50, the MLB Players' pool will receive $4. Tens of millions of dollars of income are generated this way.

Currently, each major league player, manager, and coach receives well over $100,000 in licensing fees annually. No wonder Shotgun Shuba would be willing to coach for zero salary!

THE NEW YORK YANKEES—TIGHT WITH A BUCK

The New York Yankees, baseball's most successful franchise, had the reputation of being extremely "tight with a buck"—at least until George Steinbrenner bought the team in 1973.

Take the tale of Babe Ruth, whose relations with the Yankees were strained after he retired from active play in 1935. At the beginning of the 1939 season, he wrote to the Yankees offices and requested a pair of complimentary tickets for opening day at Yankee Stadium. Ruth was curtly told by return mail that he must include his check with his request. Naturally, Ruth, who felt he was grievously insulted, was not present for opening day ceremonies.

Then we have the case of Phil Rizzuto, who often recounted this story when he was doing play-by-play for the Yankees on radio and TV. He recalled the time he hit his first homer for New York at Yankee Stadium early in 1941, his rookie season. As Rizzuto rounded third base, a fan ran onto the field, grabbed Phil's cap off the top of his head, and ran into the stands with it.

The next day Rizzuto received a note form George Weiss, Yankees general manager, saying that $5 would be deducted from his pay for losing the cap. Rizzuto said, "I couldn't help it. That fan came after me like a madman."

Weiss said firmly, "You've got to hold onto your stuff better." The $5 charge stood.

OFF THE FIELD

BAMBINO
BREAD

BABE RUTH STILL A MAJOR FORCE IN ADVERTISING

Babe Ruth still remains a force in advertising, though he passed to the "Great Beyond" more than a half-century ago. Any individual or commercial enterprise must pay his estate a royalty for using his name or image. For more than a decade, the Ruth name and image have been represented by Curtis Management, Inc., in Indianapolis, Indiana. At this point, his estate has been receiving more than $1 million dollars a year in royalties. Ruth is survived by a number of children and grandchildren, as well as by other heirs, who share in those royalties.

Ruth has even been resurrected recently in a series of food product radio commercials he "does" with Phil Rizzuto, former New York Yankees shortstop and a member of baseball's Hall of Fame. Ruth's voice is simulated by an actor, with Ruth being named in these commercials.

THE BABE RUTH UNION SUIT, A BEST-SELLER

During his long, dramatic, and tumultuous big-league baseball career, George Herman "Babe" Ruth, the Sultan of Swat, endorsed scores of commercial products, such as cigars, chewing tobacco, cigarettes, beer, meat products, various types of bread, automobiles, shirts, hats, golf clubs, baseball bats, and gloves. He also endorsed restaurants and other types of business establishments, especially those located in New York City.

Most of Ruth's advertising contracts were handled by Christy Walsh, baseball's first major agent. Walsh, an attorney and noted journalist, did not negotiate player contracts, but he became an expert in structuring endorsement contacts.

One of the most lucrative deals Walsh struck for Ruth was with McLoughlin Manufacturing Company of Kokomo, Indiana, which started in 1926—a time when the Babe was at the absolute peak of his career.

McLoughlin Manufacturing at that period was one of the country's leading producers of men's underwear, or "union suits," as they were called then. The relationship continued without interruption until Ruth's death on August 16, 1948.

The Babe Ruth portrait and facsimile signature came on all packages containing the union suits. As a result, sales zoomed because of the connection with the New York Yankees great home run hitter.

McLoughlin Manufacturing was headquartered in a sprawling red brick building in Kokomo, a town of some 50,000 population in north central Indiana on Wildcat Creek. On top of the building stood a bulbous water tower marked with an inscription reading "McLoughlin Manufacturing Company, Home of Babe Ruth Union Suits."

Crazy, but true!

Ruth was paid a royalty on every McLoughlin Union Suit endorsed by him with his photo and facsimile signature on every box. During that course of more than two decades, he earned tens of thousands of dollars in royalty payments. The endorsement contracts between Ruth and McLoughlin were renewed annually.

Barry Halper, the baseball memorabilia collector based in northern New Jersey, and part-owner of the New York Yankees, has a ring binder containing all the documents relating to the Ruth–McLoughlin deal. The documents bear the Ruth signature, together with those of Christy Walsh and McLoughlin executives. That esoteric assemblage of Ruth memorabilia today is worth a small fortune.

Babe Ruth's reputation as an American icon has grown to such great heights over the years that a near-mint package of his McLoughlin Manufacturing Company endorsed union suits is worth thousands of dollars on the current sports memorabilia marketplace.

HENRY AARON—AUTOGRAPHS, YES. REGISTRATION SIGNATURES, NO.

When anyone registers at a hotel or motel just about anyplace in the world, he must sign the registration book. But not Henry Aaron, the great home run slugger.

When Aaron appeared as an autograph guest at a show featuring all living major leaguers who had rapped out at least 3000 base hits, an event staged at Atlantic City's Showboat

Hotel and Casino in the fall of 1995, he flat out refused to sign the registry. "No way I'm going to sign that book!" Henry told the hotel clerk.

It seemed that Aaron's fee per autograph at the Showboat ranged from about $50 to more than $100, depending upon the nature of the item to be signed. (Autographed bats are the most expensive.) Henry Aaron simply wasn't going to sign anything for free.

The matter was settled when Aaron's agent signed the registry for him.

DIMAGGIO RETAINS HIS TITLE AS "THE HUMAN SIGNING MACHINE"

Joe DiMaggio, the great New York Yankees center fielder who sparkled on the diamonds for 13 seasons between 1936 and 1951 (with 3 years out for service during World War II), was named "The Greatest Living Ex-Ballplayer" at a 1969 conclave staged at the White House and hosted by President Richard M. Nixon. The event marked the centenary of professional baseball in the United States.

For the first several years of his career, DiMaggio felt he was badly underpaid by the Yankees. After having three sensational seasons, starting with his rookie year in 1936, "Joltin' Joe" held out for about 3 weeks at the start of the 1939 season in order to land a contract for $30,000—a lot of money in those days, but peanuts compared with today's boxcar salaries for star ballplayers.

By the time DiMaggio retired after the 1951 season, his salary had reached the $100,000 plateau—top money in those days, but less than each player, manager, and coach receives today through licensing agreements arranged through the Major League Players Association. (Licensing money comes from royalties for commercial use of the Major League Baseball and individual team logos. The value of the dollar has, of course, changed radically over the past half-century.)

However, whatever amount DiMaggio earned in salary in his 13-year big league career—a total that may add up to a tad over $1 million, including checks from playing in ten World Series— it pales in significance to the money he subsequently piled up as a result of his singular place in the history of the game.

Over the many years since he retired from active play, DiMaggio signed so many autographs for various fees that he became known as "The Human Signing Machine."

In our Sterling book, *Baseball Bloopers & Diamond Oddities*, published in 1991, we reported that DiMag at the time commanded the highest rate per autograph in the late 1980s—$15. Joltin' Joe was being criticized in the press for being the "Yankee Clipper," but he did not bow to derision. In response to the criticism, DiMag simply raised his rate to $18. Whenever he appeared at a "card show," fans flocked to his signing table in droves.

Through the 1990s, the DiMaggio rate for an autograph rose steadily, so that by 1999, he would command $150 to autograph a baseball, $175 for a photograph, and $350 for a Yankees cap! Thus, he had developed a "scale," according to the type of item. Autographed game-used caps brought even bigger bucks, as we'll see.

Throughout the 1980s and into the late 1990s, DiMaggio appeared at card shows staged at a variety of venues: at hotels in midtown Manhattan; at the Meadowlands Hilton in Secaucus, New Jersey; at Hofstra University based at Hempstead, Long Island; in Chicago; and at the big casino hotels in Atlantic City. In addition to his autographing fees, the show promoters also had to pay for all his travel expenses. Joe was a very sharp businessman and he knew the hold he had on the baseball fan and memorabilia collector.

Strangely enough, DiMaggio refused to sign a wide array of baseball memorabilia items for reasons only known by him. For example, at an early 1990s card show held at the Meadowlands Hilton, there was a sign at the hotel's exhibition center entrance reading:

Mr. DiMaggio will not sign the following types of items:

♦ Baseballs already signed by anyone else

♦ Original artwork portraying Mr. DiMaggio

♦ Baseball bats

♦ Baseball jerseys

On another occasion in the early 1990s, a baseball memorabilia collector traveled several hundred miles to the Meadowlands Hilton in order to have DiMaggio sign an original artwork showing him in a classic batting pose. DiMag flatly refused. The collector said in disgust, "I get on the road for hours just to have the painting signed, and DiMaggio just said, 'No.'"

DiMaggio knew that the value of the painting would multiply by some three to four times with his signature and he didn't want anyone to make an undue profit. (Pete Rose, the all-time major league base-hit king with 4256, on the other hand, will sign anything thrust down at his autograph table. We've even see Rose sign copies of *The Dowd Report*, a volume published by the Baseball Commissioner's Office that dealt with his alleged gambling on baseball. Rose is known as an "equal opportunity signer.")

DIMAGGIO'S BIG BUCKS FOR SIGNING BASEBALL BATS

While Joseph Paul DiMaggio refused to sign baseball bats at card shows, he did autograph lumber under special circumstances—and if the price was right. And DiMag's rates for bat signings were not cheap. There's something special about having a big star of the game sign a bat, especially one in the rare upper echelons in the Hall of Fame like Joe DiMaggio.

Of all of his deeds on the diamond, DiMaggio is perhaps best known for his 56-game hitting streak in 1941. Most baseball historians feel that this is one of the records that will not be broken. (Standing in second place for a consecutive hitting streak is Pete Rose, who batted safely in 44 straight games while with Cincinnati in 1978—that's the National League record.)

DiMaggio signed bats for free for fans earlier in his playing days, but he stopped that altogether when the autograph craze started taking off in early 1980s. Sometime toward the end of

1990, an ambitious promoter asked DiMaggio if he would sign 1941 bats to commemorate the 50th anniversary of his 1941 hitting streak. The promoter made DiMaggio an offer he could not refuse. He would pay the old Yankee Clipper exactly $2000 for each signed bat. The promoter then proceeded to advertise the bats at $3995 each!

DiMaggio, working in a private office, spent nearly 3 full days signing those 1941 bats. For those labors, his check came out to a little under $3.9 million. No sports person in the history of this planet has made more than $3.9 million for less than 3 days' work.

For a weekend card show, DiMaggio often cleared more than $100,000. In some cases, the promoter would take not a penny from that amount. He'd use DiMaggio as a "loss leader." The number of fans jamming into the place because of Joltin' Joe's presence would attract more business.

In the few years before his death, Joe was bringing in his own attorney to monitor these shows because he didn't want to miscount the number of autographs he signed. Remember, there was big money involved. Whenever there was a Joe D signing session, there was a big business atmosphere that breathed the "Fortune 500."

DiMaggio was also a stickler for "expenses" incurred while starring as an autograph guest at card shows. In a late 1990s card show appearance, he tacked on a $6.00 charge for taxi fare. We've got to watch those nickels!

Please don't misunderstand us, we fully appreciate Joe DiMaggio's contribution to the game of baseball and to American folklore. We interviewed this baseball great on numerous occasions and he was always a gentleman. In fact, we consider ourselves lucky because Joe didn't ordinarily grant interviews to reporters. And he was always more than happy to give us a free autograph, which we gave out to friends. Thus, we established a personal relationship with him and stand in awe at his accomplishments.

DiMaggio's strange hold upon the American sporting public was dramatically illustrated at a mid-1990s card show appearance he made at Hofstra University. The show was staged at Hofstra's cavernous Fitness Center on an early Saturday afternoon, with over 1000 people present, plus some 75 dealers, and several ex-star players autograph guests. As Joe entered the room, a sudden hush fell over the crowd as all eyes strained to get a glimpse of the former Yankee great, then past 80 with a shock of pure white hair. DiMaggio, slightly stooped and with a history of medical problems, still maintained the majestic stride of a super athlete. Fathers lifted their small sons onto their shoulders so they could get a quick look at a true baseball icon, a legend in every sense of the word. This scene was of such magnitude that it could never be forgotten.

DiMaggio always took his autograph appearance very seriously. He dressed impeccably—a tailored suit, tailored shirt, and silk tie. And even as he passed his 80th birthday, his signature remained clear and bold. He always took his time and signed carefully. Many big-time athletes just scrawl their signature at card shows.

At earlier card shows, DiMaggio would personalize any autograph, but starting in the early 1990s, he would sign his name only. At a full-fledged card show, he'd do 1000 autographs on a Saturday, and then another 1000 on Sunday; he just couldn't take the time to write out personalizations.

DIMAGGIO UNIFORM PARTS SET RECORD AT AUCTION

Anything connected with Joe DiMaggio creates serious interest and big money. For example, a public auction staged in New Jersey in March 1998 featured various pieces of equipment Joltin' Joe used during his career with the Yankees.

A pair of size 11 black spikes DiMag wore during the 1941 season was purchased for $36,094 (including the 15% buyer's premiums). The spikes took on greater value because they were autographed by DiMaggio. That figure stands as a record realization for any example of game-worn baseball spikes.

At the same auction, an autographed game-worn Yankees home pinstripe jersey worn by DiMaggio during the 1947 season realized $82,027.

Other DiMaggio items that brought hefty prices at this New Jersey auction included:

♦ a 1942 autographed game-used cap for $22,188

♦ a circa 1950 game-used bat (not autographed) for $8,630

♦ a pair of autographed circa 1950 game-used pants for $6,606

♦ a 1941 Yankee Stadium ticket from DiMaggio's 44th-hit streak game for $649

Perhaps the most unusual of all DiMaggio memorabilia specimens was offered by Sotheby's on February 29, 1992, at its sprawling New York City galleries. The item was a piece of wedding cake from DiMaggio's marriage on November 19, 1939, to actress Dorothy Arnold in San Francisco. It found a buyer at $1210, against a "modest" $500/600 estimate. The more than half-century-old hunk of wedding cake, hard as a rock and wrapped in cellophane, came with two bisque columns and a rose decoration from the cake, together with the invitation to the wedding and reception, and a photo of Joe and Mrs. DiMaggio cutting the cake!

This particular lot went to a specialist in Joe DiMaggio memorabilia who said he'd be happy to pay top dollar for anything connected with the old Yankee Clipper.

After battling a series of illnesses for several months, Joe DiMaggio died on March 8, 1999, at the age of 84 at his Florida home. As long as baseball is played, Joe DiMaggio's name will be remembered. He left us not only with an array of records and deeds achieved on the diamond, but he also left sports hobbyists with literally hundreds of thousands of baseball collectibles he had personally signed. Who knows—that figure may be well over a million.

MARK MCGWIRE'S 70TH HOME RUN BALL SELLS FOR $3,005,000 AT AUCTION

The baseball hammered out by Mark McGwire on September 27, 1998, at Busch Stadium in St. Louis for his record-breaking 70th home run, brought an incredible $3,005,000 at a public auction staged a New York City's Madison Square Garden on January 12, 1999. The hammer price came to

$2,700,000. With the auction house's commission, the total realization added up to $3,005,000.

It goes almost without saying that this marks the highest realization for any single item of baseball memorabilia sold at public auction. The winning bid was cast by Todd McFarlane, 37, a native of Calgary, Alberta, and now a resident of Tempe, Arizona. McFarlane, who claimed he spent his life's savings on this historic baseball, heads his own company, Todd McFarlane Productions, which produces a wide variety of comic books and related products. McFarlane, who is also a part-owner of the Edmonton Oilers in the National Hockey League, calls himself of "psycho baseball fan."

New official Major League baseballs, produced in a factory in Costa Rica, retail for less than $5.

IT'S ALEXANDER CARTWRIGHT, NOT ABNER DOUBLEDAY, WHO INVENTED BASEBALL!

John Sterling and Michael Kay have been partners on Yankees radio broadcasts for a decade. Although we appreciate their general knowledge of the game and its wide array of intricacies, they have their zany moments on the radio.

Michael Kay once went into a soliloquy on the beauty and symmetry of the game during a Yankees broadcast early in the 1998 season. Toward the midpoint of the game, a player hit a grounder to deep short, with the shortstop coming up with the ball and throwing in time to the first baseman to get the out. Kay in effect said, "That's beautiful... in the great majority of the cases, if an infielder handles the ball cleanly, his throw to first will get the batter out. The space between the bases, 90 feet apart, is just perfect. Thank you, General Doubleday, for inventing this great game."

The only problem with Kay's analysis is that General Abner Doubleday did not invent the game at Cooperstown, New

York, in 1839, where the first ballgame was supposed to have been played. It has been proven that Doubleday (1819–1893) never set foot in Cooperstown and had nothing to do with the development of baseball. Even historians at the Hall of Fame in Cooperstown agree, although Doubleday's mistaken connection with the diamond game is legendary.

Credit for the development of modern baseball, as we know the game, must go to Alexander Joy Cartwright (1820–1892), who organized the first baseball team, the Knickerbocker Ball Club of New York City, in 1845. Cartwright's Knickerbockers played the first organized game on June 19, 1846, at the Elysian Fields, Hoboken, New Jersey, against a club called the New Yorks.

It was Cartwright, an engineer and New York City volunteer fireman, who set the basic rules of the game that stand today; including ending the practice of putting a man out by hitting him with a thrown ball. He introduced the nine-man team with an unalterable batting order, a nine-inning game, three outs per side, and a 90-foot baseline. He also dressed his team, made up of local firefighters, in the game's first uniforms. Most New York teams of that era came out of various firehouses. Barry Halper, the indefatigable New Jersey memorabilia collector, has a wide array of Cartwright materials, including his fireman's hat and fireman's horn!

For his contributions to baseball, Alexander Cartwright was inducted into the Hall of Fame in 1938. Though there is a Doubleday exhibit in the Hall of Fame, Abner Doubleday was never elected into baseball's shrine.

The next time Michael Kay muses about the wonder of the 90-foot baselines, he should say instead, "Thank you, Mr. Cartwright."

CATCHING BASEBALLS THROWN OFF OF TALL BUILDINGS

Charles "Gabby" Street, who gained fame first as Walter Johnson's "personal catcher" with the Washington Senators and later as a pennant-winning manager of the St. Louis Cardinals in 1930–1931, is destined to be best remembered for an offbeat stunt performed in the nation's capital on the morning of August 21, 1908.

Prompted by a bet between two local sportsmen, Street won a $500 prize and worldwide publicity by catching a baseball thrown by Johnson from the top of the 555-foot high Washington Monument. Though considerably jarred by the impact of the ball as it landed in his glove, it wasn't enough to keep him from catching Walter Johnson's 3–1 victory over the Detroit Tigers that afternoon. It was said that Street's experience on the receiving end of Johnson's "cannonballs" had uniquely prepared him to accomplish the feat at the Washington Monument.

Several years later, Brooklyn Dodgers manager and former catcher Wilbert Robinson was supposed to catch a baseball thrown from the top of a newly-built New York City skyscraper. Prankster Casey Stengel, a young Brooklyn outfielder, substituted a large grapefruit for a baseball. Robinson made the catch but he was furious when he found himself covered with grapefruit pulp.

In mid-season 1938, Cleveland Indians back-up catcher Hank Helf caught a ball thrown from near the top of the 708-foot Terminal Tower (then America's tallest skyscraper outside New York City). Helf made the catch, and today his name is still remembered for that performance.

Baseballs dropped from the height of skyscrapers travel more than 150 miles an hour when they reach the ground. That type of stunt has, for all intents and purposes, been banned by Major League Baseball as being too dangerous.

"SPLASHY" NEW BALLPARK INNOVATIONS

The Arizona Diamondbacks, based in Phoenix, became the National League's newest franchise in 1998 by going all out in making their new Diamondbacks Stadium one of the most innovative ballparks ever. Chief among the innovations is a swimming pool, together with an adjacent hot tub, beyond the outfield barriers. The pool area is housed in a special sec-

tion of Diamondbacks Stadium. For a half-dozen seats or so, plus access to the pool and its accessories, fans pay more than $4000 for season reservations. The fans can also catch some rays on a suntanning deck and, if they want, watch a little baseball.

The Tampa Bay Devil Rays, the American League's newest franchise, which also debuted in 1998, took second place to no one in ballpark innovations when they opened Tropicana

Field. This way, fans who get bored with baseball can go down to a stadium super-mall underneath the outfield stands and shop for everything from shoes and shirts to new cars.

The San Francisco Giants, who hope to open a new ballpark in time for the start of the 2000 season, also plan a variety of innovations. Chief among these are: a food court, a performance cooking center, and a kid's interactive learning center.

In the *Wall Street Journal* Sam Walker commented on the new era ballpark phenomena: Critics contend that all the sideshows won't build a true fan base and once the novelties wear off, some operators will lose money. Nevertheless, team owners see it differently; they say the added attraction will lure new groups to the stadiums and prompt them to stay, spend all day, and spend a little money.

LEW BURDETTE CHANGES PITCHING ARM

Lew Burdette, who spent most of his 18-year big league career toiling for the Milwaukee Braves, and who won three games against the New York Yankees in the 1957 World Series to clinch the World Championship for the Braves, was always known as something of a prankster in his playing days. For his 1959 Topps Chewing Gum card, Burdette, a right-handed pitcher, grabbed teammate Warren Spahn's glove and tricked the Topps photographer by posing as a southpaw.

ZANY BASEBALL CARDS: GLENN HUBBARD
AND HIS PET PYTHON

In a 1998 survey, the weekly *Sports Collectors Digest* named the 1984 Fleer specimen showing Atlanta Braves second baseman Glenn Hubbard with his favorite pet, a 9-foot python, draped around his neck and shoulders, as the zaniest/wackiest baseball card. Hubbard seems to be enjoying the friendship of his reptilian friend, for he has a broad smile on his face. The python, a healthy-looking specimen, obviously has been well fed.

ROSTER